THE
BEST OF
TV
COOKERY

D1581611

THE BEST OF TV COOKERY

CONTENTS

CHAPTER 1
THE ENTERTAINERS

CHAPTER 2
THE NATURALS

First published 1986 by Octopus Books Ltd
59 Grosvenor Street, London W1

This edition © Hennerwood Publications Ltd

All illustrations © Octopus Books Ltd
For text © details see page 144

ISBN 086273 277 8

Printed in England

CHAPTER 3
AT HOME

CHAPTER 4
AND ABROAD

INTRODUCTION

Television cookery is justly popular with viewers, managing to combine all those elements of drama, colour and information that go to make a good, watchable programme. It has a wide-ranging appeal: kitchen novices can learn the basics of cutting, measuring and mixing, experienced cooks can collect new recipes and original serving ideas and enjoy comparing their methods with those of the professionals.

TV cooks need a high degree of skill – and a fair amount of courage. Cooking is, for most of us, an essentially private activity, where minor mistakes can be disguised and disasters hidden. Cooking in public, when the camera will pick up any false move and millions will witness the smallest mistake, and giving an interesting and informative running commentary at the same time, takes a particular sort of confidence and *panache*.

This book brings together the top TV cooks, many of them household names, all with a great deal to contribute to the know-how of the kitchen. They come from all walks of life: there are restaurateurs, teachers, journalists, housewives, an actress and a vicar but they all have an infectious enthusiasm for cooking. The recipes, which range from simple dishes to please the family on a restricted budget to exotic recipes to grace the most elaborate table, have been chosen to illustrate the special style of each of the cooks.

The Entertainers are those who have taken so naturally to television that their broadcasts are always stamped with their individual personalities. They enjoy entertaining, both on the screen and off, and their recipes are designed to make an impression on their guests. Whether they are creating exotic flavours, combining unusual ingredients or presenting first-class produce in eye-catching ways, they are always interesting and imaginative, often innovative and even daring. They offer an array of interesting appetizers, showpiece main courses and delicious desserts to help you create menus for the most special of special occasions.

The Naturals are the cooks who have boosted our awareness of fresh foods and urged us to make the most of natural, easily available ingredients. The emphasis here is on re-awakening jaded taste buds to the delights of fresh vegetables and fish, pulses and nuts and showing that expensive meat dishes are by no means essential to the success of a meal. Tempting vegetarian recipes quickly dispel the myth that non-meat cookery is bland and boring; fish recipes bring back the near-forgotten art of real sea-food cookery; uncooked foods are simple to prepare and good to eat. Natural foods fit well into the current view that healthy eating means cutting down on animal fats and high levels of salt and sugar contained in processed foods and including more fibre in the regular diet. A healthier diet can mean cutting the risk of heart disease, high blood pressure, diabetes and obesity – which has to be good news for all of us.

In the At Home section, the TV cooks offer the classic recipes, those once handed down from mother to daughter, in the days before convenience foods invaded the kitchen. Old-fashioned farmhouse fare, regional specialities that will come as a pleasant surprise outside their own locality, and new ideas that will extend any home cook's repertoire make up the recipes. They include substantial meals for budget-conscious families as well as special treats, pies and puddings, teatime cakes and even preserves – home cooking at its delicious best.

Television cookery programmes do not confine themselves to English and continental cookery; in recent years interest in eastern cookery has grown enormously and television has proved an excellent medium for introducing viewers to the ingredients and methods of Chinese and Indian cookery. Leading experts on Chinese cuisine have shown how they achieve a harmonious balance between

6

colour, flavour, texture and aroma, all preserved by careful preparation and brief cooking time. In the section on Cooking from Abroad there are recipes to enable you to lay on a sumptuous Chinese banquet with a variety of subtly flavoured dishes. As a contrast, Indian cooking makes liberal use of spices and it is their balance and blend that give each dish its individual taste. Indian cuisine is one of the oldest and most sophisticated in the world and the all-embracing word 'curry' cannot begin to describe the wide variety of Indian dishes and their accompaniments which the keen cook can master.

All the cooks featured in this book share a love of good food and a wish to communicate and pass on their skills. Their programmes have taken the mystique out of fine cooking; seeing dishes prepared from the first slice of onion to the final garnish convinces viewers that they, too, can succeed every time in the kitchen. Readers of these recipes can be equally confident. There is no more severe testing ground for recipes than television. Many great chefs who can produce splendid food have trouble passing on their recipes because their results so often depend on adding a pinch of this or that at whim or adjusting quantities as they go along. TV cooks have to convert feel and flair into clear instructions and exact measures so you can be sure that all the wrinkles have been well and truly ironed out.

Whether your taste runs to stuffed squid and pheasant breasts, onion pie and bread and butter pudding or Peking duck and toffee apples you will find that there are a whole range of dishes to please you. However many cookery books you own, you are sure to find this a new and fascinating addition to your collection.

7

JOHN TOVEY

AVOCADO ON TOMATO PROVENÇALE SAUCE WITH LEMON HONEY DRESSING

Serves 4

●

2 avocados, halved, stoned
and skinned
Lemon and honey dressing:
1 egg
50 g (2 oz) caster sugar
juice and rind of 1 lemon
2 tablespoons honey
300 ml (½ pint) double
cream
Tomatoes Provençale:
50 g (2 oz) butter
2 medium onions, finely
chopped
450 g (1 lb) tomatoes,
skinned, de-pipped and
roughly chopped
2 garlic cloves crushed with
1 teaspoon salt

Preparation time: 20 minutes
Cooking time: 35 minutes

Buy avocados naturally ripe
if they are to be used that
day but if they are hard
when purchased wrap them
in a newspaper and keep
them in a warm place till
ripe. I find the easiest way
to skin and prepare them is
as follows – always use a
stainless steel or silver knife
and simply cut through
them from top to bottom
going right in to the firm
stone found in the middle.
The pear should easily fall
into two halves and the
large stone come out with
no trouble. I get a large
silver tablespoon and scoop
out the whole flesh of each

has been proprietor of the Miller Howe hotel on Lake
Windermere in the Lake District, where he delights
guests with his gourmet menus, since 1971. He often
demonstrates his original and unusual dishes on television and runs cookery courses and competitions at
Miller Howe and writes for the catering press. His
early career was at the Foreign Office; later he ran a
theatrical company before his interest in good food
took over. His books include *Entertaining with Tovey,
Table Talk with Tovey* and *Feast of Vegetables.*

---

half in one fell swoop – so
much easier than fiddling
around with a knife trying
to skin it.
1. Make the dressing: mix
the egg, sugar, lemon and
honey together in a pud-
ding basin, place it over a
pan of simmering water and
cook for about 10-15
minutes, stirring occasionally with a wooden spoon
until the mixture thickens.
Leave to cool.
2. When cooled, pass the
mixture through a fine
plastic sieve and whip it
into the cream.
3. While it is cooling, make
the Tomatoes Provençale:
Melt the butter in the
saucepan and lightly fry the
chopped onions with the
crushed garlic then add the
chopped tomatoes. Cook
uncovered until the mix-
ture is thick and fairly dry,
stirring from time to time.
Allow to cool.
4. To assemble, put a
generous portion of the
cold Tomato Provençale on
four plates, and on to this
put an avocado half, cavity
down, then liberally spoon
over it at the last minute the
cold lemon dressing.

*From the left: Avocado on
Tomato Provençale sauce with
Lemon honey dressing; Chilled
Tomato soup with Lime sorbet*

8

CHILLED TOMATO SOUP

Serves 4

●

100 g (4 oz) butter
225 g (8 oz) chopped onions
1 kg (2 lb) tomatoes
including stalks if possible
1 generous bunch of mint
150 ml (¼ pint) sherry
1.2 litres (2 pints) milk

Preparation time: 10 minutes
Cooking time: 55 minutes

This cold soup can be made into a rather grand dish by putting a dollop of Lime Sorbet (next recipe) in the middle!

1. In a saucepan cook the onions in the melted butter until golden brown and then throw in the tomatoes, stalks and all. Add the mint (including stalks) and the sherry, cover with a double thickness of dampened greaseproof paper and simmer away – stirring from time to time – for forty five minutes. At this stage the tomatoes should have fallen and be mushy.
2. When cooling add the cold milk and then liquidise the soup and pass it through a sieve into a clean bowl.
3. Chill overnight and serve with sprigs of fresh mint or with some of the Lime Sorbet, if liked.

LIME SORBET

Serves 4

●

600 ml (1 pint) cold water
175 g (6 oz) cube sugar
juice and rind of 2 fresh
limes
1 egg white

Preparation time: 15 minutes,
plus freezing
Cooking time: 12 minutes

Lime Sorbet does go very well with the Chilled Tomato Soup and is also extremely pleasant served in small glasses as a course prior to the main one.
1. Put the water, sugar and limes into a perfectly clean saucepan, bring to the boil and then simmer for 12 minutes.
2. Pass through a sieve into a receptacle and, when cold, put in the freezer compartment of your fridge.
3. When frozen solid it can be removed and either broken up and put into a modern food processor or beaten back to a slushy consistency with an electric hand beater. In a separate bowl, lightly beat an egg white until frothy, fold this into the smooth slushy sorbet and return to the freezer to set. 150 ml (¼ pint) of cream makes the sorbet a richer dish.

CASSEROLE OF CHICKEN, PIG'S TROTTERS AND VEGETABLES

Serves 4
●

300 ml (½ pint) strong clear chicken stock
600 ml (1 pint) inexpensive dry white wine
150 ml (¼ pint) sherry
350 g (¾ lb) assorted root vegetables finely and evenly diced
finely chopped herbs of choice – parsley, mint, chives, tarragon, basil, thyme
1 fresh 1½ kg (3 lb) chicken
salt
freshly ground black pepper
2 small pig's trotters

Preparation time: 40 minutes
Cooking time: 1½ hours
Oven: 180°C, 350°F, Gas Mark 4

Definitely one of my favourite chicken dishes as it is easy to do and is superb for a picnic with the family, the highlight being the lovely diced vegetables that become set in the pig's trotter jelly! Make sure you have a casserole large enough to take all the ingredients.

1. Pour the stock, white wine and sherry into the casserole and add the chopped vegetables and herbs. Be generous with the salt and pepper both inside and on the outside of the fresh chicken and then place this breast down in the casserole. Split open the two small pig's trotters and press these down the side of the chicken.

2. Put on the hob and bring up to the boil. Immediately remove to preheated oven and cook with the lid on for 1½ hours.

3. Remove from oven and leave to cool with lid covered.

From the left: Casserole of chicken, pig's trotters and vegetables; Ham cooked with treacle and beer

HAM COOKED WITH TREACLE AND BEER

Serves 10-12

●

1 ham weighing 2.3/4 kg (6 lb)
6 tablespoons molasses or dark black treacle
cloves
demerara sugar
900 ml (1½ pints) lager or light ale

Preparation time: 40 minutes
Cooking time: 2½ hours
Oven: 190°C, 375°F,
Gas Mark 5

Ham is a tasty dish served hot or cold; once, dozens of local places prospered on Fried Ham and Egg high teas.

1. Put the ham in a large pan, cover with cold water and leave in a cool place for 48 hours, changing the water every morning and evening, four times in all.

2. Boil the ham gently in a fresh change of water, to which you have added the molasses, or treacle, for 2 hours. Allow to cool, then remove it from the water.

3. Using a sharp knife, cut away the skin to reveal the soft fat. Mark the fat with criss-cross incisions and push a clove in the centre of each diamond. Coat the whole fat surface generously with demerara sugar. Place the ham in a roasting tin.

4. Put the lager or ale into a saucepan and heat through. Pour it into the roasting tin and put the tin in the preheated oven. Roast for 30 minutes. Serve hot or cold.

JOHN TOVEY

THE ENTERTAINERS

11

MILLER HOWE UTTER BLISS

Serves 2

●

1 small melon
100 g (4 oz) strawberries or raspberries
1 tablespoon brandy
2 tablespoons icing sugar
approx half bottle sparkling white wine, chilled
2 tablespoons redcurrants

Preparation time: 30 minutes

This is an excellent starter for a summer's evening – particularly if you can get fresh redcurrants.

1. Slightly top and tail the melon before cutting it into two around the middle. This 'topping and tailing' will balance the portion better, but don't take huge slices off, otherwise the filling will run out. Remove the seeds.

2. Scoop out balls from all around the edge of the melon with a medium-sized parisian scoop or melon baller. Return the balls to their 'home', bottoms up. Place the melon halves on a tray, cover well and leave until required.

3. Meanwhile, liquidize the strawberries or raspberries with the brandy and icing sugar and leave to chill.

4. At the last minute, put the redcurrants into the well of the melon, lightly pour round the 'balled' rim the liquidized strawberries and fill the well to the brim with the sparkling wine.

Variation:
If you cannot find redcurrants, fresh, stoned cherries are delicious too.

AMERICAN CHOCOLATE WHEATMEAL SLICE WITH BUTTERSCOTCH SAUCE

Serves 6

●

225 g (8 oz) soft butter
4 large fresh eggs
225 g (8 oz) soft brown sugar
5 teaspoons baking powder
4 tablespoons cocoa
2 tablespoons dark rum
225 g (8 oz) wheatmeal flour
Filling:
600 ml (1 pint) double cream
2 tablespoons dark rum
2 tablespoons caster sugar
Butterscotch sauce:
450 g (1 lb) golden syrup
100 g (4 oz) caster sugar
100 g (4 oz) demerara sugar
100 g (4 oz) soft butter
150 ml (¼ pint) double cream

Preparation time: 30 minutes, plus cooling
Cooking time: 45 minutes
Oven: 180°C, 350°F, Gas Mark 4

If you are fortunate enough to have a food processor, your task will be the easier as the machine does everything for you.

This mixture will fill a 28 cm (11 inch) square cake tin; if yours is smaller it will take a little longer to bake and if larger not quite so long!

1. Make the cake: beat everything together and put into a cake tin lined with greaseproof paper and bake in a preheated oven for approximately 30 minutes.

2. Test with a knitting needle or similar object to see if cooked. Remove from the oven and allow to cool. When the slice is cool and you wish to make up the sweet, turn it out on to a work surface and carefully remove the greaseproof paper. Cut straight down the middle and then each of these two sections again in half through their middle. Thus you will have four layers to pile up to make the loaf-like looking slice.

3. Beat the filling ingredients together to a thick consistency and spread three of the slices with the mixture. Place the slices on top of each other, the plain one on the top.

4. To serve, slice through as if cutting a loaf and lay a slice on each plate.

5. Make the sauce: stir all the ingredients together except the cream over a medium heat until they form a runny sauce then carry on cooking for about 12 minutes, stirring from time to time.

6. Remove from the heat and beat in the cream little by little and keep on beating for about 5 minutes.

7. Pour over the wheatmeal slice or when cool put into 2×450 g (1 lb) jam jars as the sauce keeps for some time. It is lovely with ice cream, cold apple pie or poached peaches.

Variation:
Use 4 tablespoons of Camp Coffee instead of the powdered cocoa in the mixture.

From the left: Miller Howe utter bliss; American chocolate wheatmeal slice with Butterscotch sauce

12

JOHN TOVEY

THE ENTERTAINERS

13

REV. JOHN ELEY

VIRGIN MARY'S SOUP

Serves 4-6

•

900 ml (1½ pints) chicken stock
75 g (3 oz) fresh breadcrumbs
4 hard-boiled egg yolks
1 cooked chicken breast, skinned and boned
75 g (3 oz) blanched almonds
150 ml (¼ pint) double cream
salt
white pepper
white bread croûtons, to garnish

Preparation time: 10 minutes
Cooking time: 20 minutes

---

the 'Cooking Canon', is vicar of a large Midlands parish and has been a regular contributor to *Pebble Mill At One* since 1980. Since his childhood in Suffolk, where his father was a shepherd, he has enjoyed working in the kitchen and began cooking on television as a result of contributing to the *Sherborne Abbey Cookery Book* while he was a curate. His cookery books, *Entertaining With The Cooking Canon* and *Simply Divine*, written with Rabbi Lionel Blue, have both been in the best-seller lists.

---

1. Put 300 ml (½ pint) of the stock in a saucepan with the breadcrumbs and bring to the boil.
2. Pour the stock mixture into a blender or food processor, and add the egg yolks, cooked chicken and blanched almonds. Blend this mixture until it is very smooth.
3. Add the cream, and salt and pepper to taste. Blend again.

4. Pour the mixture into the top of a double boiler and heat it gently over simmering water.
5. Heat the remaining stock and add to the chicken mixture. Continue heating gently, stirring occasionally, until piping hot. Do not allow to boil as the soup could curdle.
6. Serve the hot soup in individual bowls and garnished with the croûtons.

CRAB MOUSSE

Serves 4-6

•

1 sachet powdered gelatine
3 tablespoons water
120 ml (4 fl oz) mayonnaise
juice of 2 lemons
juice of 2 limes
1 tablespoon Dijon mustard
pinch of ground mace
25 g (1 oz) fresh parsley, coarsely chopped
25 g (1 oz) fresh chives, coarsely chopped
150 ml (¼ pint) soured cream
450 g (1 lb) crabmeat
3 egg whites
salt
white pepper

Preparation time: 15 minutes plus chilling

14

1. Dissolve the gelatine in the warm water, then blend with the mayonnaise, which should be at room temperature or above. Whisk in the lemon and lime juices, mustard and mace.
2. Add the parsley, chives, soured cream and crabmeat and fold in thoroughly.
3. Whisk the egg whites until stiff but not dry, and fold into the mixture with salt and pepper to taste.
4. Spoon the mixture into a buttered mould or dish, or into individual crab-shaped moulds. Chill until set and serve garnished with lemon or lime slices, if liked.

PHEASANT BREASTS IN A PORT WINE SAUCE

Serves 4

●

4 pheasant breasts, skinned and wiped
25 g (1 oz) plain flour
75 g (3 oz) butter
1 teaspoon dried thyme or 1 dessertspoon fresh thyme, finely chopped
1 wineglass port
1 wineglass game stock
175 g (6 oz) mushrooms, finely chopped
juice of 1 lemon
finely grated rind of ½ lemon
salt
freshly ground black pepper

Preparation time: 10 minutes
Cooking time: 30-40 minutes

1. Coat the pheasant breasts in flour, shaking off excess, and set them aside. Blend the remaining flour with 50 g (2 oz) of the butter and the thyme.
2. Heat the thyme butter in a heavy pan and add the pheasant breasts. Cook gently, turning occasionally, until browned all over and almost cooked, about 20-30 minutes. Remove the pheasant breasts and place in a warm oven, covered with foil.
3. Add the port to the pan and bring to the boil. Set alight and swirl the juices around gently until the flames die down. Add the stock and simmer gently for a few minutes to reduce the sauce.
4. Meanwhile, sprinkle the mushrooms with the lemon juice and leave to macerate.
5. Add the lemon rind to the sauce. Add the mushrooms and juice and stir well. Cook for about 1 minute. Swirl in the remaining butter, and add salt and pepper to taste.
6. Pour the sauce over the pheasant breasts and serve.

From the left: Virgin Mary's soup; Crab mousse; Pheasant breasts in a port wine sauce

REV. JOHN ELEY

THE ENTERTAINERS

15

PIGEON PIE

Serves 6

•

6 oven-ready pigeons
1 onion, peeled and halved
1 carrot, peeled and sliced
1 bouquet garni
1 wineglass red wine
150 ml ($\frac{1}{4}$ pint) water
350 g (12 oz) shortcrust
pastry
25 g (1 oz) butter
1 large red pepper, cored,
seeded and diced
2 teaspoons cayenne
pepper
25 g (1 oz) flour
beaten egg to glaze

Preparation time: 45 minutes
Cooking time: 1$\frac{1}{4}$ hours
Oven: 190°C, 375°F,
Gas Mark 5

---

1. Cook the pigeons, onion, carrot, bouquet garni, wine and water in a large pressure cooker – for 20 minutes.
2. Strain off the stock and reserve. Remove the breasts from the pigeons; use the rest of the birds for another recipe. Remove all skin and bone from the breasts and set aside.
3. Roll out two-thirds of the pastry and use to line a medium pie dish. Layer the pigeon breasts in the dish.
4. Heat the butter in a small pan, add the red pepper and cook until soft. Stir in the cayenne pepper and flour, then gradually stir in the reserved stock. Bring to the boil, stirring until thickened.
5. Pour the sauce over the pigeon breasts in the pastry case. Roll out the remaining pastry and use to cover the pie. Flute the edges and decorate the top. Glaze with beaten egg.

6. Place in a preheated oven and bake for 40 minutes or until golden brown.

CHICKEN APRICOT PEPPER

Serves 6

•

25 g (1 oz) butter
6 chicken joints
1 onion, peeled and finely
chopped
450 g (1 lb) dried apricots,
soaked, cooked and puréed
600 ml (1 pint) chicken
stock
2$\frac{1}{2}$ teaspoons green
peppercorns
25 g (1 oz) cornflour
salt

Preparation time: 10 minutes
plus soaking
Cooking time: 1$\frac{1}{4}$ hours

---

1. Melt the butter in a flameproof casserole, add the chicken joints and brown them all over. Remove from the pan.
2. Add the onion to the casserole and cook until softened. Stir in the apricot purée, stock and peppercorns and bring to the boil.
3. Return the chicken joints to the pan and simmer gently for about 45 minutes.
4. Transfer the chicken joints to a warmed serving dish and keep hot.
5. Dissolve the cornflour in a little cold water and add to the cooking liquid.

Simmer, stirring, until thickened. Taste and add a little salt.
6. Pour the sauce over the chicken and serve.

From the top: Chicken apricot pepper; Pigeon pie

SUNDAY SPECIAL LEG OF LAMB

Serves 4-6

●

25 g (1 oz) butter
2 tablespoons oil
1 large onion, peeled and chopped
2 large carrots, chopped
2 head chicory, chopped
3 celery stalks, chopped
1.5-2 kg (3-4 lb) leg of lamb
450 g (1 lb) smoked back bacon
6 fresh rosemary sprigs
225 g (8 oz) apricot jam
300 ml (½ pint) chicken stock
salt
freshly ground black pepper

Preparation time: 25 minutes
Cooking time: 1¾-2¼ hours
Oven: 190°C, 375°F,
Gas Mark 5

1. Heat the butter and oil in a frying pan, add all the vegetables and cook until softened.
2. Meanwhile, make 6 deep incisions in the lamb, cutting right down to the bone. Into each incision, push a bacon rasher and a sprig of rosemary.
3. Tip the vegetable mixture into a roasting tin and spread it out. Place the lamb on top of the vegetables. Arrange the remaining bacon rashers over the lamb to cover it.
4. Melt the apricot jam in a small saucepan and ladle it over the lamb. Pour the stock over the vegetables, and add salt and pepper to taste.
5. Place in a preheated oven and roast, allowing 25 minutes to each 450 g (1 lb) plus 25 minutes over.
6. When the lamb has finished cooking, the jam will have turned black, but don't worry. That is what is meant to happen. Place the lamb on a warmed serving platter and remove the blackened bacon. Keep hot.
7. Strain off the cooking juices into a saucepan and thicken with a little cornflour, if liked.
8. Arrange the vegetables around the lamb and serve with the delicious gravy in a sauce boat.

Sunday special leg of lamb with a gravy of cooking juices

SARAH'S MANGO CHILL

Serves 4-6

•

4 egg yolks
100 g (4 oz) caster sugar
few drops of vanilla essence
600 ml (1 pint) milk
2 large ripe mangoes
150 ml (¼ pint) double cream

Preparation time: 20 minutes plus chilling

---

1. Beat the egg yolks with the sugar and vanilla essence until light and fluffy. Heat the milk in a heavy saucepan until almost boiling, then whisk half of it into the egg mixture. Pour this mixture back into the pan and cook gently, stirring, until the custard thickens enough to coat the back of the spoon.
2. Allow the custard to cool for about 1 hour.
3. Meanwhile, peel the mangoes and cut the flesh away from the stone. Purée the flesh in a blender or food processor.
4. Stir the mango purée into the custard. Whip the cream until thick and fold it in.
5. Divide the mixture between dessert glasses and chill well before serving.

Clockwise from the top: Mère Catherine; Sarah's mango chill; Strawberry marquise

STRAWBERRY MARQUISE

Serves 4

•

450 g (1 lb) strawberries
1 pineapple
1 tablespoon caster sugar
1 measure Kirsch
450 ml (¾ pint) double cream
1 egg white
25 g (1 oz) caster sugar

Preparation time: 25 minutes, plus marinating and chilling

---

1. Wash and hull the strawberries and cut them in half. Cut the pineapple in half, remove the woody core and purée the flesh from one half. Cut the other half into small cubes. Mix the hulled strawberries and the pineapple cubes and pour over the measure of Kirsch. Sprinkle the tablespoon of caster sugar on the top and allow to marinate for a couple of hours.
2. Lightly whip the cream and fold in the puréed pineapple. Whisk the egg white until stiff and fold in the sugar. Now gently fold together the pineapple cream and the egg white.
3. Place most of the halved strawberries and pineapple cubes into a serving dish with the juices, keeping a few strawberries back. Top with the pineapple cream and decorate with the strawberries. Allow to chill before serving.

MÈRE CATHERINE

Serves 6-8

•

200 g (7 oz) white chocolate
4 egg yolks
100 g (4 oz) caster sugar
450 ml (¾ pint) double cream
chopped nuts
orange liqueur

Preparation time: 30 minutes plus freezing

---

1. Break the chocolate into a bowl placed over a pan of hot water and melt it. Allow to cool slightly.
2. Beat the egg yolks with the sugar until light and fluffy. Heat the cream in a heavy saucepan until almost boiling, then whisk half of it into the egg mixture. Pour this mixture back into the pan and cook gently, stirring, until the custard thickens enough to coat the back of the spoon.
3. Remove from the heat and stir in the melted chocolate. Allow to cool.
4. Pour the mixture into an ice cream maker and freeze. Alternatively, freeze the mixture in a bowl and whisk it once or twice during the freezing process to prevent ice crystals forming.
5. Scoop out balls of ice cream with an ice cream scoop and roll them in warmed nuts to coat all over. Cover and freeze again until required.
6. Just before serving, arrange the ice cream balls on a plate or dish and pour over some warmed liqueur. Set alight and serve immediately while flaming.

REV. JOHN ELEY THE ENTERTAINERS

MICHAEL SMITH

PRAWN, MANGE-TOUT AND CAULIFLOWER SALAD

Serves 4-6
●

$\frac{1}{2}$ cucumber
2 avocados
lemon juice
2 oranges, peeled and segmented
450 g (1 lb) cooked Mediterranean prawns, peeled
900 ml (1$\frac{1}{2}$ pints) chicken stock
$\frac{1}{2}$ lemon
$\frac{1}{2}$ small cauliflower, broken into small florets
100 g (4 oz) mange-tout, stringed if necessary
1 tablespoon chopped fresh chives or parsley
To garnish:
watercress
4-6 cooked prawns in shell
Dressing:
1 teaspoon dry mustard
1 garlic clove, peeled and crushed
1 teaspoon finely grated orange rind
150 ml ($\frac{1}{4}$ pint) olive oil
2 tablespoons wine vinegar
1 teaspoon caster sugar
salt
freshly ground black pepper

Preparation time: 40-45 minutes plus chilling
Cooking time: 3$\frac{1}{2}$ minutes

---

1. Using a canelle knife, take strips of skin lengthways from the cucumber (or peel it entirely). Cut the cucumber in half lengthways and scoop out the seeds. Cut each half crossways into 5 mm ($\frac{1}{4}$ inch)

is well-known as cookery presenter in *Pebble Mill At One* and for his countrywide lectures and demonstrations. He created the food for the long-running TV series *Upstairs Downstairs* and *The Duchess of Duke Street* and designed three of London's most prestigious restaurants: Walton's, The English House and The English Garden. His publishing successes include *Cooking with Michael Smith* and *Fine English Cookery* and his BBC publications have sold more than a quarter of a million copies.

thick slices. Chill.
2. Peel and stone the avocados. Cut them into 5 mm ($\frac{1}{4}$ inch) thick slices lengthways and sprinkle with lemon juice to prevent discoloration. Cover and chill.
3. Chill the oranges and prawns, in separate containers.

4. Bring the stock to the boil in a saucepan. Squeeze in the juice from the $\frac{1}{2}$ lemon, then add the lemon. Add the cauliflower florets and cook for 1$\frac{1}{2}$ minutes. Remove with a slotted spoon and cool, then chill.
5. Meanwhile bring the stock back to the boil and add the mange-tout. Sim-

mer for 2 minutes, then drain and cool under running cold water. Chill.
6. Combine all the dressing ingredients in a screw-topped jar and shake well.
7. When ready to serve, put all the prepared ingredients in a large bowl and pour over the dressing. Toss well.
8. Divide between individual dishes and sprinkle over the chives or parsley. Garnish with sprigs of watercress and prawns in shell.

Clockwise from the top: Walton's oeufs en cocotte; Salmon and peach mayonnaise; Prawn, mange-tout and cauliflower salad

20

SALMON AND PEACH MAYONNAISE

Serves 4-6

●

2 tablespoons olive oil
1 tablespoon lemon juice
1 tablespoon chopped fresh
chives, tarragon or mint
salt
freshly ground black
pepper
450 g (1 lb) cooked salmon
fillet, skinned and flaked
2 ripe peaches, skinned,
stoned and sliced, or 4
canned peach halves, sliced
150 ml (¼ pint)
mayonnaise
curly lettuce leaves

Preparation time: 30 minutes

1. Combine the olive oil, lemon juice, herbs and salt and black pepper to taste in a bowl.
2. Add the prepared salmon and mix gently into the dressing. Add 2 or 3 of the peach slices to the mixture.
3. If the mayonnaise is very thick, thin it with a little water.
4. Arrange the fish mixture on a serving platter and pour over the mayonnaise to coat it.
5. Garnish the dish with the remaining peach slices and bouquets of curly lettuce leaves.

WALTON'S OEUFS EN COCOTTE

Serves 6

●

15 g (½ oz) butter
1 teaspoon finely chopped
shallot or onion
175 g (6 oz) sweetbreads,
blanched, skinned and
diced
pinch of curry powder
salt
freshly ground black
pepper
5 tablespoons double cream
6 large eggs
2 slices of crustless white
bread, made into crumbs
6 teaspoons grated
Parmesan cheese

Preparation time: 25 minutes
Cooking time: about 15 minutes
Oven: 200°C, 400°F,
Gas Mark 6

1. Melt the butter in a small pan, add the shallot or onion and cook until softened. Add the sweetbreads and fry for 1-2 minutes. Sprinkle over a good pinch of curry powder, and salt and pepper to taste.
2. Stir in the cream. Simmer for 3-4 minutes or until the sweetbreads are tender.
3. Divide the sweetbread mixture between 6 cocottes, measuring 7.5 cm (3 inches). Break an egg into each cocotte and season with salt and pepper. Sprinkle with the breadcrumbs and cheese.
4. Stand the cocottes on a baking sheet and place in a preheated oven. Bake for 5-6 minutes or until the eggs are just set. Serve hot.

MICHAEL SMITH THE ENTERTAINERS

21

FILLETS OF SOLE IN RED WINE

Serves 4

•

8 Dover sole fillets, skinned and wiped
salt
freshly ground black pepper
50 g (2 oz) field mushrooms, finely chopped
25 g (1 oz) finely chopped onion
red wine (see below for amount to use)
½ chicken stock cube
75 g (3 oz) unsalted butter
25 g (1 oz) plain flour

Preparation time: 25 minutes
Cooking time: about 25 minutes

1. Select a shallow pan large enough to hold the folded fillets in one layer.
2. Gently bat the fillets with a wet rolling pin to flatten them. Season the fish with salt and pepper. Fold each fillet in half.
3. Scatter the mushrooms and onion over the bottom of the pan and arrange the fillets on top, in one layer. Pour over enough red wine just to cover. Put a buttered piece of greaseproof paper on top.

4. Bring to the boil, then reduce the heat and simmer for 6-7 minutes.
5. Remove the fillets to a warmed serving platter, cover with a clean damp cloth to prevent them drying out and keep warm.
6. Add the stock cube to the cooking liquid and stir to blend. Boil rapidly until the liquid is reduced by half, then strain it into a small saucepan.
7. Blend 25 g (1 oz) of the butter with the flour to make a smooth paste. Add this beurre manié to the simmering sauce in small pieces, whisking. Add just enough beurre manié to

thicken the sauce.
8. Cut the remaining butter into 1 cm (½ inch) cubes. Remove the pan from the heat and whisk in the cubes of butter. The sauce will increase in volume and be light and buttery.
9. Pour the sauce over the fish and serve immediately.

Fillets of sole in red wine

COQ AU VIN

Serves 4-6

•

75 g (3 oz) butter
2 tablespoons olive oil
50 g (2 oz) lean belly pork, diced
1 onion, peeled and chopped
1.5-2 kg (3-4 lb) roasting chicken, cut into 4 pieces
1 sherry glass of brandy
red wine (Burgundy or Beaujolais)
1 fresh bouquet garni (1 celery stalk, 4 parsley stalks, 1 sprig of thyme and 1 large bay leaf tied together)
2 garlic cloves, peeled and crushed
salt
freshly ground black pepper
50 g (2 oz) tiny button mushrooms
25 g (1 oz) flour
chopped fresh parsley or tarragon, to garnish

Preparation time: 15 minutes
Cooking time: 1 ¼ hours

---

1. Heat 50 g (2 oz) of the butter and the oil in a pan just large enough to contain the chicken pieces. Add the pork and onion and fry until browned. Remove with a slotted spoon.
2. Add the chicken pieces and brown well on all sides. Pour over the brandy and set alight. Pour in enough red wine just to cover the chicken pieces, and add the pork, onion, bouquet of herbs and garlic. Add salt and pepper to taste.
3. Simmer for 45 minutes, removing the breasts when they are cooked and leaving the thighs longer if necessary. Remove the chicken to a warmed serving dish.
4. Add the mushrooms and simmer for 5 minutes.
5. Make a beurre manié (paragraph 7, opposite) and

add only enough to thicken the liquid to the consistency of single cream.
6. Pour the mushrooms and sauce over the chicken and sprinkle with parsley or tarragon. Serve hot.

GIGOT QUI PLEURE

Serves 6-8

•

2.25 kg (5 lb) leg of lamb
2 large garlic cloves, peeled and cut into thin slivers
50 g (2 oz) butter
1 teaspoon dried thyme
1 teaspoon powdered bay leaf or dried rosemary
2 tablespoons olive oil
6 potatoes, peeled and thinly sliced
4 onions, peeled and thinly sliced
600 ml (1 pint) stock
salt
freshly ground black pepper

Preparation time: 20 minutes
Cooking time: about 1 ½ hours
Oven: 230°C, 450°F, Gas Mark 8

---

1. Make incisions in the lamb, about 4 cm (1½ inches) deep, at 5 cm (2 inch) intervals, all over the top side of the leg. Insert a sliver of garlic into each incision.
2. Rub the butter and herbs all over the lamb. Stand the leg in a roasting tin and spoon over the oil.
3. Place in a preheated oven and roast for 30 minutes.
4. Meanwhile, mix the potatoes and onions together in a large bowl, adding salt and pepper to taste.
5. Remove the lamb from the roasting tin. Layer the potatoes and onions in the fats in the roasting tin and pour over the stock.
6. Return the tin to the oven on a lowish shelf. Slide in the next shelf immediately over the tin and place the lamb on this so that its juices will drip into the vegetables as the roasting continues. Continue to roast the lamb for a further hour (or more if you like it very well done). You may have to reduce the temperature if the lamb starts to burn, but you should have quite a good roasting noise going on.
7. When cooking is completed, the lamb should be done to your taste, and the vegetables tender and full of the meat flavours.

MICHAEL SMITH · THE ENTERTAINERS

23

RICH PEAR TART

Serves 6-8
●

Pastry:
100 g (4 oz) plain flour
40 g (1½ oz) ground
almonds
1 egg yolk
75 g (3 oz) unsalted butter,
softened
50 g (2 oz) caster sugar
¼ tsp vanilla essence
Filling:
1 egg yolk
75 g (3 oz) caster sugar
50 g (2 oz) ground almonds
2 tablespoons Kirsch
3 large ripe pears
3 eggs
300 ml (½ pint) single
cream

*Preparation time: 45 minutes,
plus chilling
Cooking time: about 50 minutes
Oven: 220°C, 425°F,
Gas Mark 7; then
190°C, 375°F,
Gas Mark 5; then
180°C, 350°F,
Gas Mark 4*

1. To make the pastry, sift the flour into a bowl and stir in the almonds. Tip on to a work surface and make a well in the centre. Put in the remaining pastry ingredients and mix with the fingertips to a rich dough. Chill for 1 hour.

2. Roll out the dough and use to line a 20 cm (8 inch) deepish flan ring. Place in a preheated oven and bake blind for 10 minutes, then reduce the temperature and bake for a further 10 minutes.

3. Meanwhile, cream the egg yolk with 50 g (2 oz) of the sugar. Add the ground almonds and 1 tablespoon of Kirsch and beat well.

4. Peel, halve and core the pears. Put them in a bowl, sprinkle over the remaining Kirsch and turn to coat to prevent discoloration.

5. Spread the almond mixture over the bottom of the pastry case. Arrange the pear halves on top in a ring with their pointed ends to the centre.

6. Beat the eggs well with the remaining sugar. Stir in the cream. Pour over the pears.

7. Reduce the oven temperature once again. Bake the tart until the filling has set. Serve hot or warm.

From the left: Christmas pudding; Rich pear tart

24

CHRISTMAS PUDDING

Makes 2 × 1.75 kg (4 lb) puddings

•

350 g (12 oz) cold unsalted butter
225 g (8 oz) plain flour
225 g (8 oz) fresh brown breadcrumbs
225 g (8 oz) ground almonds
350 g (12 oz) sultanas
350 g (12 oz) raisins
350 g (12 oz) whole glacé cherries
50 g (2 oz) candied angelica, chopped
100 g (4 oz) crystallized or dried apricots
100 g (4 oz) crystallized or bottled chestnuts
450 g (1 lb) muscovado sugar
6 eggs, beaten
grated rind and juice of 1 lemon
grated rind and juice of 2 oranges
600 ml (1 pint) sweet brown ale such as barley wine
6 tablespoons Bénédictine

Preparation time: 30 minutes
Cooking time: 5 hours, then 3 hours

---

1. Grate the butter on the coarse side of the grater.
2. Combine all the dry ingredients in a large mixing bowl. Add the butter.
3. Mix together the eggs, lemon and orange rinds and juices, ale and Bénédictine. Add to the dry ingredients and mix well.
4. Put into buttered basins, cover with foil, and steam. Cool and store.
5. On the day of eating, steam the Christmas pudding for a further 3 hours.

MICHAEL SMITH THE ENTERTAINERS

GLYNN CHRISTIAN

PRAWNS WITH PERNOD AND KIWI FRUIT

Serves 4-6

•

6 kiwi fruit, peeled
2-3 dessertspoons Pernod
4 dessertspoons
mayonnaise
finely grated rind and juice
of 1-2 limes
225 g (8 oz) peeled cooked
prawns
small spinach leaves
radicchio
finely grated lime rind, to
garnish

---

*Preparation time: 25 minutes
plus chilling*

---

1. Cut each kiwi fruit into 6 segments lengthways. Place in a bowl and sprinkle over the Pernod. Cover and chill for at least 30 minutes.
2. Mix the mayonnaise, lime rind and juice. Chill.
3. If the prawns were frozen, pat them dry with paper towels.
4. To assemble the dish, put a few layers of spinach leaves and radicchio at the bottom of seafood cocktail glasses. Add the kiwi fruit and then the prawns and top with the lime mayonnaise. Alternatively, the ingredients may be arranged on a serving plate, with the kiwi segments to look like sun rays and the prawns piled up in the middle.
5. Sprinkle with a little more grated lime rind and serve cool but not too cold.

Left and front: Prawns with Pernod and kiwi fruit; right top: Dill-pickled salmon with mustard eggs

began demonstrating his innovative skills as a television cook on *Pebble Mill At One* in 1982 and he entertained BBC2 viewers with his *Cook's Tour* of Venice, Egypt, Greece, Turkey and Israel. Since the beginning of BBC's *Breakfast Time* he has appeared three times a week as chef and food reporter. Born in Auckland, New Zealand, he is a great-great-great-grandson of Fletcher Christian. He came to Britain in 1965 and worked for several years as a travel writer before opening a London delicatessen called Mr Christian's.

DILL-PICKLED SALMON WITH MUSTARD EGGS

Serves 6

•

1 kg (2 lb) tail piece of
salmon or sea trout
90 g (3 oz) sugar
90 g (3 oz) salt
20 white peppercorns,
coarsely crushed
2 bunches of fresh dill
fronds
Mustard eggs:
6 small eggs
2-3 tablespoons cream or
milk
25 g (1 oz) butter
2 tablespoons whole grain
mustard

---

*Preparation time: 30 minutes
plus chilling
Cooking time: 3-4 minutes*

---

1. Bone the salmon, or have your fishmonger do this, to make 2 fillets. Be sure all small bones are removed, and scrape off the scales.
2. Mix together the sugar, salt and peppercorns.
3. Select a deep dish in which the salmon can lie flat, and scatter one-quarter of the seasoning mixture over the bottom. Strew one-quarter of the dill fronds over the bottom,

then place one piece of salmon on top, skin side down. Scatter over another quarter of the seasoning mixture and dill. Press one-quarter of the seasoning mixture and dill on to the flesh side of the second piece of salmon and lay it on top of its partner, flesh to flesh. Cover with the remaining seasoning mixture and dill.
4. Put a plate or dish on top of the fish and weight it. Refrigerate for 48 hours, turning the fish over every 6 hours, more or less.
5. To make the mustard eggs, lightly beat the eggs with the cream or milk. Melt the butter in a heavy pan and cook the eggs, stirring, until beginning to scramble. Add the mustard and fold rather than stir the eggs to make long, velvety curds. Remove from the heat whilst the eggs are still very soft. Allow to cool, then chill.
6. To serve, scrape the dill and peppercorns from the salmon (the salt and sugar will have dissolved in the juices) and cut the fish into the thinnest possible slices. Slice towards the tail, angling the knife downwards so that each slice takes a little flesh from the skin, thus avoiding waste.
7. Serve with the mustard eggs.

TROUT WITH CELERIAC AND HAZELNUT STUFFING

Serves 4
•

4 trout, 250-350 g (8-12 oz) each
450 g (1 lb) celeriac, peeled
2-3 tablespoons lemon juice
1-2 garlic cloves, peeled and crushed
100 g (4 oz) hazelnuts, toasted and chopped
4 tablespoons white wine or vermouth
40 g (1½ oz) butter, cut into small pieces
soured cream, to serve (optional)

Preparation time: 30 minutes
Cooking time: 15 minutes
Oven: 180°C, 350°F, Gas Mark 4

1. Bone the trout, if liked.
2. Grate the celeriac into a bowl in which you have put the lemon juice. (The juice will prevent the celeriac from discolouring.) Add the garlic and hazelnuts and mix together well.
3. Extend the cavity in each fish right to the tail and fill with the stuffing.
4. Lay the trout on buttered foil, in one layer, and sprinkle with the wine or vermouth. Dot with the butter. Wrap the foil around the fish and seal well. Place on a baking sheet.
5. Bake in a preheated oven for 15 minutes.
6. For the nicest presentation, remove the skin on the top side of each trout and dot on some blobs of soured cream.

LAMB CHOPS ON TOAST

Serves 4
•

4 medium-thick slices of wholemeal bread
whole grain mustard, such as Moutarde de Meaux
fresh mint leaves or dried mint
4 double lamb chops

Preparation time: 10 minutes
Cooking time: 20 minutes
Oven: 180°C, 350°F, Gas Mark 4

1. Spread each slice of bread generously with mustard, then cover with a good layer of mint. Put a chop on top and curl in its ends, trimming if you have to do so.
2. Transfer to a baking sheet and place in a preheated oven. Cook for 10 minutes, then turn the chops over. Cook for a further 10 minutes. This will give you pink flesh, so cook a little longer if you prefer it more well done.
3. Serve hot.

Clockwise from top right: Trout with celeriac and hazelnut stuffing; Lamb chops on toast; Chicken breasts in lime coconut sauce

CHICKEN BREASTS IN LIME COCONUT SAUCE

Serves 4
•
75 ml (3 fl oz) fresh lime juice
50 ml (2 fl oz) dry white vermouth
25 g (1 oz) fresh root ginger, peeled
4 skinless, boneless chicken breasts (suprêmes)
1 small green chilli, seeded and thinly sliced
200 g (7 oz) creamed coconut, chopped
finely grated rind of 1 lime

Preparation time: 15 minutes, plus marinating time
Cooking time: 35-45 minutes
Oven: 180°C, 350°F, Gas Mark 4

---

1. Pour the lime juice and vermouth into a mixing bowl. Add the juice from the ginger, using a garlic crusher, and stir.

2. Arrange the chicken breasts in a baking dish. Pour over the lime juice mixture and sprinkle over the chilli. Leave to marinate for 2-3 hours, turning from time to time.

3. Cover the dish and place in a preheated oven. Bake for 30-40 minutes.

4. Strain off the cooking juices into a saucepan. Keep the chicken hot.

5. Add the coconut to the juices and heat gently, stirring. Do not boil or the sauce will curdle.

6. Pour this sauce over the chicken and sprinkle with the lime rind. Serve hot.

GLYNN CHRISTIAN THE ENTERTAINERS

29

EARL GREY'S SORBET WITH ORIENTAL FRUITS

Serves 6-8

•

25 g (1 oz) Earl Grey tea
leaves
550 ml (1 pint) boiling
water
150 g (5 oz) caster sugar
3-4 tablespoons lime or
lemon juice
1-2 egg whites (optional)
Oriental fruits:
lychees, peeled and
sprinkled with rosewater
fresh dates, peeled, stoned
and soaked in vodka
slices of tangerine
slices of kumquat
kiwi fruit, peeled, sliced
and sprinkled with
Cointreau

---

*Preparation time: 25 minutes
plus freezing*

---

1. Put the tea leaves into a
bowl and pour over the boiling water. Leave to steep for
7 minutes, then strain into a
measuring jug. Add cold
water to bring the liquid
quantity back up to 550 ml
(1 pint) if necessary.
2. Add the sugar to the
strained tea and stir until
dissolved. Add lime or
lemon juice to taste.
3. Pour the liquid into a
freezer container and freeze
for 1 hour or until set at the
edges and mushy in the
centre.
4. Tip the sorbet into a
bowl and beat well to break
down the ice crystals. Alternatively, use a food processor which will add air and
lighten the sorbet.

5. Whisk the egg whites
until stiff but not dry and
fold into the sorbet. Return
to the container and freeze
until solid.
6. About 30 minutes before
serving, transfer the sorbet
to the refrigerator to allow
it to soften slightly.
7. Serve with the fruits.

HELLO SAILOR! BREAD AND BUTTER PUDDING

Serves 4-6

•

6-8 slices white toast,
buttered
2-3 teaspoons ground
cinnamon
1 very ripe banana
50 g (2 oz) raisins or
sultanas
grated rind and juice of 1
lime
2 eggs
3 tablespoons sugar, brown
or white
6 tablespoons dark rum
600 ml (1 pint) milk

---

*Preparation time: 20 minutes,
plus sitting time
Cooking time: 50 minutes
Oven: 180°C, 350°F,
Gas Mark 4*

Choose almost any white
bread other than that from
a sliced sandwich loaf, as
this will become a nasty
mush.

1. The toast should be
lavishly buttered and
sprinkled with the cin-
namon. Remove the crusts
and slice the toast into

even-sized fingers.
2. In a small bowl, slice the
banana, mix in the raisins
or sultanas, and add the
lime rind and juice. Mix
well. Beat the two eggs together, then add the sugar,
rum and milk.
3. Arrange the spicy toast
and the fruit in layers in an
oblong or square baking
dish, remembering that the
bread will swell. Pour in the
custard mixture and let this
sit for 20-30 minutes, gently
pushing the top layer under
the liquid from time to time

until all is absorbed. Then
pour over any remaining
lime juice from the
banana/raisin mixture.
4. Bake in a preheated
oven for 50 minutes, or until the custard is set and the
toast is crisp and golden on
top. Serve warm rather than
hot, with lashings of cream
flavoured with more rum.

Hot Jaffa Mousse Souffle

Serves 6

●

20-22 sponge fingers
175 g (6 oz) dark, sweet chocolate
100 g (4 oz) unsalted butter
6 eggs, separated
6 teaspoons grated orange rind
6 tablespoons orange juice

Preparation time: 25 minutes
Cooking time: 30 minutes
Oven: 190°C, 375°F,
Gas Mark 5

1. Butter a 1.5 litre (2½ pint) soufflé dish. Line the sides of the dish with the sponge fingers, cutting off the ends as necessary, and placing the sponge fingers sugar side out. Crumble the cut-off bits of biscuit and spread them over the bottom of the dish.

2. Gently melt the chocolate and butter together, then pour into a mixing bowl. Add the egg yolks and orange rind and juice and whisk together well.
3. Beat the egg whites until stiff but not dry and fold into the chocolate mixture.
4. Spoon the mixture into the biscuit-lined dish. Place in a preheated oven and bake for 30 minutes. The soufflé will be nicely risen with a runny middle. Serve at once decorated with slivers of orange rind, if liked.

From the left: Earl Grey's sorbet with oriental fruits; Hello sailor! bread and butter pudding; Hot jaffa mousse soufflé

GLYNN CHRISTIAN THE ENTERTAINERS

31

DISH SALAD

Serves 1

•

Chinese leaves, chopped
celery sticks
carrot sticks
green and red pepper,
cored, seeded and cut into
rings
few slices of fennel
few slices of baby turnip
some mange-tout, topped
and tailed
some apple slices
red onion slices
radish roses
small bunch of grapes
watercress
parsley
1 orange
handful of chick-pea
sprouts
Tofu Dip, Dracula's
Delight or Creamed
Carrot (see below)

Preparation time: 25 minutes

---

1. Line the serving bowl with the Chinese leaves. Push the celery and carrot sticks into the pepper rings and arrange on the Chinese leaves with the fennel, turnip, mange-tout, apple, onion, radish roses, grapes, watercress and parsley.
2. Cut the orange down through the centre into segments, leaving them attached at the base. Peel back the skin from the segments so they can be removed easily from the base of the orange.
3. Place the orange in the centre of the salad and sprinkle over the sprouts. Serve with one of the dip-dressings, Tofu Dip, Dracula's Delight, or Creamed Carrot, which follow this recipe.

extolled the merits of a diet high in uncooked vegetables, fruit, seeds and nuts in their best-seller *Raw Energy*. Their television series and the accompanying book *Raw Energy Recipes*, showed the variety of delicious recipes used in their family's high-raw diet. Leslie Kenton, the mother of four children, is the daughter of American jazz musician Stan Kenton and became health and beauty editor of *Harpers and Queen* 16 years ago. She treats food as an essential part of a complete beauty and fitness routine.

TOFU DIP

•

225 g (8 oz) tofu
juice of one lemon
1 tablespoon wholegrain
Meaux mustard
¼ crumbled vegetable
bouillon cube
1 tablespoon chopped fresh
basil
1 tablespoon chopped fresh
mint

Preparation time: 1 minute

---

1. Combine all the ingredients well in a blender or food processor until they form a smooth dip.

DRACULA'S DELIGHT

•

1 small beetroot
75 g (3 oz) sunflower seed,
toasted or raw
juice of two lemons, plus 1
tablespoon grated lemon
rind
2 tablespoons tamari
good pinch of cayenne
pepper
pinch dried thyme or 1
teaspoon chopped fresh
thyme
water, to mix

Preparation time: 5 minutes

---

1. Scrub and grate the beetroot.
2. Combine in a blender or food processor with all the other ingredients, plus enough water to give the desired consistency and blend well, adjusting the seasoning to taste.

CREAMED CARROT

•

2 carrots, roughly chopped
225 g (8 oz) tofu or cream or
cottage cheese
25 g (1 oz) walnuts
2 tablespoons chopped
parsley
1 pinch grated nutmeg
¼ vegetable bouillon cube,
crumbled
water or carrot juice, to thin
sliced carrots, to garnish

Preparation time: 10 minutes

---

1. Blend the carrots well in a blender or food processor with the tofu or cheese and nuts.
2. Add the herbs and seasonings and water or juice to thin.

3. Serve sprinkled with carrot slices.

FRESH GREEN SOUP

Serves 4-6

•

2 avocados
450 ml (¾ pint) apple juice
225 ml-450 ml (8-15 fl oz)
water
1 heaped teaspoon chopped
lemon rind
juice of 2 lemons
1 teaspoon vegetable
bouillon powder
parsley
fresh lovage
dash of white wine
centre stalks of a head of
celery, chopped with the
leaves
lemon slice to garnish

Preparation time: 10 minutes

---

1. Peel and stone the avocados. Put the flesh into a food processor and add the apple juice, 225 ml (8 fl oz) water, the lemon rind and juice, bouillon, herbs and wine. Blend until smooth.
2. Add the celery and blend again well.
3. Thin the soup to the desired consistency with the remaining water.
4. Serve garnished with a lemon slice.

Centre: Dish salad with Tofu dip, Dracula's delight and Creamed carrot dip dressings; top: Fresh green soup

SEED AND NUT CHEESES

•

100 g (4 oz) nuts, e.g. cashews, almonds, pecans
150 g (5 oz) seeds, e.g. sunflower, pumpkin
175-225 ml (6-8 fl oz) water
1 teaspoon vegetable bouillon powder
Sage and onion:
2 spring onions, finely chopped
6 fresh sage leaves, finely chopped, or 1 teaspoon dried sage
2 tablespoons wine
Garlic and herb:
2 tablespoons chopped mixed fresh herbs
1 garlic clove, peeled and crushed
juice of ½ lemon

Preparation time: 15 minutes plus maturing

1. Blend the nuts and seeds finely in a food processor.
2. Add the water and bouillon powder and blend to a firm paste.
3. Divide the mixture in half. Mix one half with the sage and onion seasonings, and the other half with the garlic and herb seasonings. Pack the two cheeses into dishes.
4. Cover with a tea towel and leave at room temperature for several hours, then refrigerate.
5. Use as a spread on vegetable and fruit slices or on savoury biscuits.

SANDSTONE LOAF

Serves 4
•

6 carrots, roughly chopped
3 celery stalks, roughly chopped
juice of ½ lemon
25 g (1 oz) blanched almonds
40 g (1½ oz) pumpkin seeds
2 tablespoons tahini
½ onion, peeled and finely chopped
handful of fresh parsley, chopped
2 teaspoons vegetable bouillon powder
1 tablespoon grated beetroot
Garnish:
parsley leaves
unblanched almonds

Preparation time: 15 minutes

1. Put the carrots and celery in a food processor and add the lemon juice. Blend thoroughly, then scrape into a mixing bowl.
2. Grind the nuts and seeds well in the food processor, and add to the bowl.
3. Add the tahini, onion, parsley, bouillon and beetroot and mix well.
4. Pack the mixture into a loaf tin. Garnish with parsley and almonds.

From the left: Sandstone loaf; Seed and nut cheeses; Garden crunch salad; Carrot juice, Cucumber and apple juice, Grape juice

GARDEN CRUNCH SALAD

Serves 1
•

½ iceberg lettuce, shredded
2-3 broccoli heads and stalks
100 g (4 oz) red cabbage, finely shredded
2-3 tomatoes, chopped
several mushrooms, sliced
handful of fresh peas
1 shallot or small red onion, peeled and cut into rings
handful of toasted pumpkin seeds
mayonnaise

Preparation time: 15 minutes

1. Place the lettuce in a salad bowl.
2. Break the broccoli florets into small pieces; peel the stems and slice them crossways. Add to the bowl.
3. Add the cabbage, tomatoes, mushrooms, peas and shallot or onion. Toss all the ingredients together.
4. Sprinkle the top with the pumpkin seeds.
5. Serve with a thinned mayonnaise dressing.

34

Raw Juices

Fresh pressed apple, grape or carrot juice is like nectar from the gods compared to the bottled variety you can buy. And raw juices have remarkable healing properties, being exceptionally rich in health-producing enzymes as well as vitamins, minerals and trace elements useful in restoring biochemical balance to the body.

Raw juices cannot be made in a food processor or blender. They require a special juice extractor – usually a centrifuge affair into which you feed the fruits and vegetables as it chops them and spins out their precious juices. Then you are left with the juice which you drink and the pulp which you toss into the compost. The health-promoting properties of fresh juices depends on their being drunk live – that is within a few minutes of being made – so that the oxidation processes which sets in almost immediately does not destroy essential vitamins and enzymes.

CARROT An excellent juice for alkalinising the system and therefore for countering stress. It is rich in carotene which the body turns into vitamin A – an important nutrient in protecting you from infection and early ageing.

CUCUMBER This juice is a natural diuretic – it encourages your body to get rid of excess water stored in the tissues. We prefer cucumber juice mixed with, say, apple or carrot or both, since its taste is slightly insipid.

GRAPE This juice is famous not only for its deliciousness but also for its natural sugars which are traditionally considered ideal for a short spring-clean regime. Warning: once you have tasted real fresh grape juice you will never again be content with the bottled variety!

Raspberry Fruit Freeze Pie

Serves 4

•

175 g (6 oz) stoned dried
dates
50 g (2 oz) unblanched
almonds
50 g (2 oz) rolled oats
1 teaspoon honey
Filling:
2 bananas, peeled and cut
into 2.5 cm (1 inch) pieces
225 g (8 oz) raspberries
dash of sherry
honey (optional)

---

*Preparation time: 20 minutes
plus freezing*

---

1. Grind the dates and
almonds as finely as pos-
sible in the food processor.
Add the oats and honey and
blend again.
2. Gradually add a little
water, just enough to bind
the mixture without
making it sticky.
3. Press the mixture into a
pie pan using your fingers.
Set aside.
4. Put the banana pieces
and raspberries into a
freezer bag and freeze until
firm.
5. Blend the fruits together
with the sherry and a little
honey to sweeten, if liked.
6. Pour the filling into the
pie shell and serve im-
mediately, decorated with a
few banana slices or raspberries, if liked.

Orange Sorbet

Serves 4

•

8 juicy seedless oranges
honey
grated nutmeg or ground
ginger (optional)
1-2 peaches, peeled, stoned
and grated (optional)

---

*Preparation time: 5 minutes plus
freezing*

---

1. Squeeze the juice from 6
of the oranges into a food
processor. Peel the remaining oranges and quarter
them; add to the processor.
Add enough honey to
sweeten and some spice, if
liked, and blend well.
2. Add the grated peach to
give the sorbet texture, if
liked.
3. Pour the mixture into
ice cube trays and freeze.
4. About 10 minutes before
serving, remove the sorbet
from the freezer and leave it
to thaw slightly.
5. Blend the sorbet again
and serve immediately.

STUFFED PINEAPPLE SALAD

Serves 4

●

1 large pineapple
1 orange, peeled and sliced
1 mango or papaya, peeled,
stoned or seeded and
chopped
100 g (4 oz) raspberries or
strawberries
2 fresh figs, finely chopped
desiccated coconut, to
decorate

Preparation time: 15 minutes

---

1. Cut the pineapple in half lengthways, through the green crown. Remove the flesh from each half, leaving shells about 1 cm (½ inch) thick. Dice the pineapple flesh, discarding the hard core.

2. Mix the pineapple with the orange, mango or papaya, raspberries or strawberries (cut in half if large) and figs.

3. Fill the pineapple shells with the fruit mixture and sprinkle the tops with a little coconut, if liked.

Left, top: Orange sorbet; left, bottom: Raspberry fruit freeze pie; right: Stuffed pineapple salad

LESLIE & SUSANNAH KENTON

THE NATURALS

37

SARAH BROWN

HARRIRA (MOROCCAN SOUP)

Serves 8

•

50 g (2 oz) chick peas, soaked overnight
50 g (2 oz) butter beans, soaked overnight
50 g (2 oz) black-eyed beans, soaked overnight
50 g (2 oz) red kidney beans, soaked overnight
50 g (2 oz) large green lentils
50 g (2 oz) yellow split peas
50 g (2 oz) green haricot beans
400 g (14 oz) tin peeled tomatoes
225 g (8 oz) onions, coarsely chopped
¼ teaspoon black pepper
1 teaspoon turmeric
½ teaspoon powdered ginger
1 teaspoon cinnamon
2 tablespoons lemon juice
1½ teaspoons salt
1½-2 tablespoons flour
1 large bunch of fresh coriander or parsley, finely chopped
a few sprigs of mint, finely chopped, or 2 teaspoons dried mint
1 teaspoon paprika
a good pinch cayenne (optional)
50 g (2 oz) tiny pasta shapes or rice (optional)

Preparation time: 15 minutes, plus soaking
Cooking time: 3½ hours

1. Drain the beans and put them back in the saucepan with 1.2 litres (2 pints) of water and simmer them for 1½ hours.

in her BBC television series *Vegetarian Kitchen* and its accompanying book dispelled any idea that vegetarian meals are dull and tasteless and provided plenty of recipes for committed vegetarians and those who want to experiment with non-meat meals. She was originally a dancer and drama teacher but when she became a vegetarian she opened her own wholefood shop and later a vegetarian restaurant and bakery in Scarborough. In 1982 she became Director of the Vegetarian Society's Cookery School.

2. Add the rest of the pulses, onions, tomatoes chopped up small with their juice, pepper, turmeric, ginger, cinnamon and lemon, but not the salt (or the beans will take longer to cook). Boil fast for 10 minutes and then simmer for another hour. Add the salt when the beans are tender, and about 1.2 more litres (2 pints) of water.
3. Add 1½ tablespoons of cold water to the flour and mix it to a paste. Beat in a few ladlefuls of broth and pour this back into the soup, stirring vigorously. Continue to stir until the soup is bubbling again and has thickened without leaving any lumps. The flour gives the soup a texture which the Moroccans call 'velvety' and which they usually achieve by stirring in leavened dough left over from bread making.
4. Simmer the soup until the beans are soft. Add the herbs, paprika and cayenne and, if you like, pasta or rice and cook for about 15 minutes until these are done. Add water if the soup is too thick.

CREOLE PATE WITH SPICED FRUIT SALAD

Serves 6

•

For the pâté:
100 g (4 oz) uncooked red lentils
1½ tablespoons oil
1 teaspoon ground cumin
½ teaspoon turmeric
½ teaspoon ground coriander
½ teaspoon mustard powder
225 g (8 oz) onions, peeled and finely chopped
2 tablespoons smooth peanut butter
juice of half a lemon
100 g (4 oz) ground roasted peanuts
salt
freshly ground black pepper
good pinch chilli powder
For the spiced fruit salad:
1 fresh green chilli, seeded and finely chopped
3 tablespoons olive oil
2 teaspoons white wine vinegar
salt
freshly ground black pepper
4 slices pineapple, fresh or tinned, diced
1 red or green pepper, seeded and diced
1 banana, peeled and sliced
1 avocado, peeled and diced

Preparation time: 45 minutes, plus chilling

1. Spread the lentils out on a plate and pick out any tiny stones or ungerminated seeds, then wash them well in a sieve under the cold tap. Put in a saucepan with the 900 ml (1½ pints) water and bring to the boil, skimming off any scum that forms. Add a teaspoon of oil and cook the lentils gently for 15 minutes until quite soft. If still moist, dry out over a low heat, stirring constantly, until the mixture becomes fairly firm. Drain and set aside.
2. Heat a tablespoon of oil in a pan, add the spices and cook until you can smell a good aroma. This takes about 3-5 minutes. Then add the onion and cook gently for 10 minutes over a low heat, stirring occasionally. Add the cooked lentils and mix them in thoroughly. Transfer the mixture to a bowl and beat in the peanut butter, lemon juice and ground peanuts. Add salt, freshly ground black pepper and chilli powder to taste. The mixture will be fairly creamy at this point, but if you put it into a lightly oiled dish, it will firm up when chilled and can even be turned out.
3. To make the salad, put the chilli into a bowl, then add the oil, vinegar and seasoning and stir vigorously with a fork. Toss the remaining ingredients in this dressing and chill for 30 minutes before serving.

From the top: Harrira; Creole pâté with spiced fruit salad

SARAH BROWN ▌▌▌▌ THE NATURALS

39

VEGETABLE MOUSSAKA

Serves 4

•

50 g (2 oz) green or brown
lentils
600 ml (1 pint) water
4 tablespoons oil,
preferably olive
1 onion, peeled and
chopped
1 garlic clove, crushed
100 g (4 oz) mushrooms,
wiped and chopped
2-3 tablespoons tomato
purée
2 teaspoons dried oregano
1 teaspoon freshly grated
nutmeg
salt
freshly ground black
pepper
350 g (12 oz) or 2 medium
aubergines, washed and
sliced
2 potatoes, scrubbed,
boiled and sliced
2 tomatoes, washed and
thickly sliced
For the sauce:
20 g (¾ oz) butter
1 tablespoon flour
250 ml (8 fl oz) milk
1 small egg
½ teaspoon mustard
powder
salt
freshly ground black
pepper
75 g (3 oz) grated Cheddar
cheese

---

*Preparation time: 1 hour 20
minutes
Cooking time: 40 minutes
Oven: 180°C, 350°F,
Gas Mark 4*

When I lived in the Sudan,
aubergines were very much
part of the staple diet, start-
ing with aubergine jam for
breakfast and finishing with
aubergine stew at night.
This dish is one of my
favourite ways of eating
these rich-coloured vegetables and is delicious
served with steamed cour-
gettes, broccoli and a fresh
tomato sauce.
1. Pick the lentils over for
sticks and stones, wash
them thoroughly, then
bring to the boil in the
water. Cover and simmer
for 40-45 minutes or until
they are soft. When cooked,
drain and reserve the liquid
for stock.
2. Heat 2 tablespoons of oil
in a frying pan and fry the
onions and garlic gently so
that they remain trans-
lucent. Then add the
chopped mushrooms and
cooked lentils and cook for
a further few minutes,
mixing well. Remove the
vegetables from the pan
using a slotted spoon so
that as much oil as possible
is left in the frying pan.
3. Put the vegetables into a
bowl and mix in a little
stock, 2-3 tablespoons of
tomato purée and the
oregano. Season well with
nutmeg, salt and freshly
ground black pepper. Then
add 2 more tablespoons of
oil to the frying pan and fry
the aubergine slices until
soft, turning them over
constantly. (You may need
a little extra oil for this.)
Put the slices on to a piece
of kitchen paper to drain
and let them cool.
4. Grease a 1.75 litre (3
pint) ovenproof dish and
put in a layer of lentil and
mushroom mixture, then a
layer of aubergines, then of
potato and tomato slices.
5. Next make the white
sauce. Melt the butter in a
small saucepan and stir in
the flour. Cook the roux for
2-3 minutes. Pour on the
milk and bring the sauce to
the boil, stirring constantly.
Simmer for 5 minutes and
then allow to cool. Beat in
the egg and season the
sauce well with mustard,
salt and freshly ground
black pepper. Pour the
sauce over the top of the
casserole and sprinkle over
the grated cheese. Bake for
40 minutes until the top-
ping of cheese is golden
brown and bubbling. Serve
piping hot.

VEGETABLES A L'ANGLAISE

Serves 4

•

1 kg (2 lb) potatoes, peeled
100 g (4 oz) Cheddar cheese
1 onion, peeled
4 tablespoons oil
salt
freshly ground black
pepper
3 leeks, washed and finely
chopped
450 g (1 lb) carrots,
scrubbed and diced
1 small cauliflower, divided
into florets
225 g (8 oz) mushrooms,
wiped and sliced
2 teaspoons fresh parsley or
rosemary, chopped
For the topping:
100 g (4 oz) grated cheese
1 tablespoon fresh parsley,
finely chopped

---

*Preparation time: 20 minutes
Cooking time: 1 ½ hours
Oven: 180°C, 350°F,
Gas Mark 4*

The term 'à l'anglaise' is
usually defined as meaning
'cooked in a homely man-
ner', a good description of
this pie where the lightly
cooked, colourful vege-
tables piled on top of a tasty
cheese and potato crust
have a simple but fresh
appeal. It doesn't take long
to make and can be adapted
all year round according to
what vegetables are in
season. Serve with a cheese
or tomato sauce and a side
salad, or choose an ac-
companying vegetable
which contrasts with those
used in the pie.
1. Grate the raw potatoes,
cheese and half the onion
by hand or in a food pro-
cessor. Mix in 2 table-
spoons of oil and season
well. Press this mixture into
a 23 cm (9 inch) deep pie-
dish, building up the sides
to form a shell. Bake in the
preheated oven for 45
minutes until the crust is
just beginning to brown.
2. Meanwhile prepare the
vegetables. Heat the 2 remaining tablespoons of oil
and fry the remaining onion
(chopped), leeks, carrots
and cauliflower florets
slowly for 5-10 minutes,
turning them over in the
pan. Then add the sliced
mushrooms and continue
cooking all the vegetables
for a further 5 minutes with
the pan covered. Add the
herbs, salt and freshly
ground black pepper.
3. Next pile the vegetables
into the baked cheese and
potato crust and sprinkle
the grated cheese mixed
with the chopped parsley
over the top. Bake for 20
minutes until the edges of
the shell look crisp and the
cheese has melted. Serve
hot.

FLEMISH SALAD

Serves 4

●

1 head chicory
2 oranges, peeled and segmented
6 sticks celery, trimmed and cleaned and cut on the diagonal
1 bunch watercress
Blue cheese dressing
(Makes 180 ml/ ⅓ pint dressing)
1 egg yolk
150 ml (¼ pint) oil (preferably sunflower oil)
1-2 tablespoons lemon juice
50 g (2 oz) blue cheese
2 tablespoons soured cream or yogurt
1 heaped teaspoon dill, chopped
1 garlic clove, crushed
freshly ground black pepper

Preparation time: 30 minutes

The beautifully shaped leaves and colour of chicory are the basis for this classic salad. Choose heads of chicory that are mainly white in colour to get the best flavour. Both from the nutritional and visual points of view, it is best to leave the chicory blades whole. If you cut them, they will soon discolour.

1. Make the dressing: First make a mayonnaise by beating the egg yolk and adding the oil drop by drop, beating thoroughly. It is easiest to do this with an electric whisk. When half the oil is added, mix in 1 tablespoon of lemon juice. Then add the remaining oil, 1 tablespoon at a time, beating thoroughly. Add the remaining lemon juice.

Crumble or mash in the blue cheese and then stir in the soured cream or yogurt, dill and garlic. Season with plenty of freshly ground black pepper. Leave to chill.

2. Separate the blades of chicory but leave them whole. Cut the oranges into small pieces. Then mix the ingredients together and pour over the dressing. Alternatively lay out a bed of watercress and arrange the chicory blades on it like the petals of a flower. Cover these with slices of orange in a circular pattern and pile the chopped celery into the centre. Then hand the dressing around separately.

From the left: Vegetable moussaka; Vegetables à l'anglaise; Flemish salad

Rum and Raisin Cheesecake

Makes 20 cm (8 inch) round cheesecake

•

For the base:
100 g (4 oz) butter or margarine
50 g (2 oz) brown sugar
75 g (3 oz) plain wholewheat flour
75 g (3 oz) ground almonds
For the topping:
2 eggs, separated
50 g (2 oz) light raw cane sugar
175 g (6 oz) cream cheese
175 g (6 oz) curd cheese
½ teaspoon vanilla essence
100 g (4 oz) raisins soaked in 3 tablespoons rum
150 ml (¼ pint) double cream

Preparation time: 25 minutes, plus chilling
Cooking time: 15 minutes
Oven: 180°C, 350°F, Gas Mark 4

This rich cheesecake definitely belongs in the special treats category. I like to flavour it with raisins and rum but you could use other dried fruit and liqueur/spirit combinations.

1. First make the base. Cream the fat and sugar until they are light and fluffy. Then stir in the flour and ground almonds and beat the mixture to make a dough. Press the dough into a 20 cm (8 inch) round greased cake tin, preferably one with a loose, removable base. Bake for 15 minutes in a preheated oven until the base is brown and well cooked.

2. Meanwhile prepare the filling. Beat the egg yolks with 25 g (1 oz) of the sugar, then beat in the cheeses, vanilla essence and soaked raisins and rum. Whip the cream and fold it into the mixture.

3. Whisk the egg whites until they are stiff and beat in the remaining sugar. Fold the egg whites carefully into the cheese mixture. Spoon the filling over the cooled base and chill the cheesecake for 4-5 hours or overnight until it has set.

Pears Alhambra

Serves 4

•

4 pears (preferably Williams or Comice)
grated rind of 1 orange
275 ml (½ pint) sweet red wine
1 tablespoon crystallised ginger, finely chopped
25 g (1 oz) demerara sugar

Preparation time: 20 minutes
Cooking time: 20 minutes

When pears are stewed in red wine they turn a beautiful rosy colour which looks very attractive. This is delicious served with Brown Bread Ice Cream.

1. Peel the pears, leaving the stalks on if possible, and slice a small portion from the base so that they will stand upright. Bring the wine to the boil with the orange rind. Add the peeled pears and poach them gently for 20 minutes.

2. Remove them from the pan and stand them in a serving dish. Boil the remaining juice with the crystallized ginger and sugar until thick and syrupy, then spoon it carefully over the pears. Chill thoroughly and serve with cream or ice cream.

BROWN BREAD ICE CREAM

Makes 600 ml (1 pint)

●

75 g (3 oz) fresh brown
breadcrumbs
75 g (3 oz) demerara sugar
2 eggs, separated
1 tablespoon honey
450 ml (¾ pint) double or
whipping cream

---

*Preparation time: 20 minutes,
plus freezing
Cooking time: approximately
10 minutes
Oven: 190°C, 375°F,
Gas Mark 5*

This is a marvellous ice cream, easy to make and quick to freeze, which has a flavour similar to praline. It is also the best way I know of using up breadcrumbs. Serve it with the Pears Alhambra.

1. Mix the breadcrumbs and the sugar together and spread them out on a baking sheet. Bake in the preheated oven until the sugar has melted and the breadcrumbs have caramelised. (This is like making praline.) Then let them cool completely.

2. Beat the egg yolks and honey in a large bowl. Next lightly whip the cream. In a separate bowl whisk the egg whites until they are firm but not dry. Fold the cream and egg whites together and then fold them carefully into the egg yolk and honey mixture. Stir in the caramelised breadcrumbs and freeze the mixture until firm. (This takes a few hours.)

3. About 20 minutes before serving, take the ice cream out of the freezer and stand it in the refrigerator, so that it softens slightly.

From the left: Rum and raisin cheesecake; Pears Alhambra; Brown bread ice cream

43

KEITH FLOYD

FLOYD'S FISH SOUP

Serves 6
•

1 kg (2¼ lb) mixed fish, which must include gurnard or red mullet, small soft-shelled crabs, conger eel, John Dory, a handful of langoustines and a piece of dogfish
olive oil for frying
2 leeks, chopped
2 large ripe tomatoes, chopped
2 onions, peeled and chopped
2 large garlic cloves, peeled and crushed
2.25 litres (4 pints) water
1 bay leaf
1 frond fresh fennel
1 teaspoon grated orange rind
100 g (4 oz) small vermicelli
1 sachet saffron
salt
freshly ground black pepper
To serve:
rouille (see page 46)
150 g (5 oz) Gruyère cheese, grated
aïoli (see page 46)

Preparation time: 30 minutes
Cooking time: 40 minutes

---

1. Clean and wash the fish. Chop into pieces about 6 cm (2½ inches) long, head, bones and all. Set aside.
2. Heat oil in a large heavy pan and fry the leeks, tomatoes, onions and garlic until softened. Add the water and bring the saucepan to the boil.
3. Add the fish, bay leaf, fennel and orange rind. Simmer for 15 minutes.

has been a fish enthusiast since he caught his first trout at the age of 14 and in his BBC television programme and book *Floyd on Fish* he has done his best to re-introduce the joys of fresh fish to those who have forgotten. He began his career as a journalist before he joined the army and, finding the food uneatable, set out to improve it. Since the early 1960s he has run restaurants in France, Spain and England before retiring from the catering business to spend his time writing and broadcasting.

The finest prawn cocktail in the world

4. Remove the fish with a slotted spoon, and leave the soup to simmer gently. Crush or grind the fish in a blender or food processor, and return it to the soup. Stir well.
5. Strain through a fine sieve into a clean pan; discard the contents of the sieve.
6. Bring the strained soup to the boil. Add the vermicelli, saffron and salt and pepper to taste and simmer until the vermicelli is tender.
7. Serve with the accompaniments: let your guests add rouille according to their taste and grated cheese to be stirred into the soup. The aïoli is to be spread on bread and dunked in.

THE FINEST PRAWN COCKTAIL IN THE WORLD

Serves 4
•

50 g (2 oz) radicchio
25 g (1 oz) fresh, small young dandelion leaves
36 langoustines, freshwater crayfish or large prawns, freshly cooked, peeled and chilled (not frozen prawns)
350 g (12 oz) very fine French beans, cooked until just tender and chilled
12 asparagus spears, cooked and chilled
4 fennel fronds, to garnish
Pink sauce:
2 egg yolks
2 tablespoons tomato ketchup
1 tablespoon bland oil
1 tablespoon olive oil
1 teaspoon Dijon mustard
4 tablespoons mild full-fat soft cheese
salt
freshly ground black pepper

Preparation time: 30 minutes

---

1. Arrange the radicchio and dandelion leaves in a small mound on large white plates. Divide the shellfish (reserving 4 for garnish), beans and asparagus elegantly among the plates.
2. To make the pink sauce, put all the ingredients in a food processor and blend to a smooth, pourable consistency.
3. Coat the shellfish and vegetables with the pink sauce, and garnish with the reserved shellfish and fennel fronds.

MARINATED FISH WITH YOGURT AND SPICES

Serves 6

●

½ teaspoon paprika
4 tablespoons coriander
seeds
½ teaspoon salt
6 cardamom pods
2 onions, peeled and finely
chopped
2 garlic cloves, peeled
¼ teaspoon ground black
pepper
1 tablespoon chopped fresh
dill
½ green pepper, cored,
seeded and chopped
2 tablespoons chopped
fresh mint
juice of 1 lemon
175 ml (6 fl oz) plain
unsweetened yogurt
6 trout, whiting or perch,
cleaned, or 6 thick hake or
cod fillets
butter for basting

---

*Preparation time: 15 minutes
plus marinating
Cooking time: 10-20 minutes*

---

1. Place all the ingredients except the yogurt, fish and butter in a blender or food processor. Blend to a smooth paste. Mix the paste with the yogurt.
2. Spread the paste inside and all over the fish. Leave to marinate for 1 hour.
3. Cook the fish under a preheated grill, or over a wood fire, until crisp and cooked through. Turn the fish from time to time and baste with butter and the marinade.

KEITH FLOYD ▪ THE NATURALS

From the top: Bread spread with Aïoli; Floyd's fish soup; Marinated fish with yogurt and spices

45

THE NATURALS

KEITH FLOYD

ROAST MONKFISH WITH GARLIC

Serves 4

●

1 kg (2¼ lb) piece monkfish tail
1 bulb plump garlic, as fresh as possible
1 tablespoon olive oil
¼ teaspoon fresh thyme leaves
¼ teaspoon fennel seeds
juice of 1 lemon
salt
freshly ground black pepper
1 bay leaf

Preparation time: 10 minutes
Cooking time: about 25 minutes
Oven: 220°C, 425°F,
Gas Mark 7

1. Skin the fish carefully, leaving no trace of the thin membrane under the skin, and remove the central bone. Rinse and pat dry, then tie up the fish with string like a piece of meat.
2. Peel 2 cloves of garlic and cut into thin slices. Make some incisions in the fish and insert the garlic slices.
3. Heat the oil in a frying pan and brown the fish on all sides for about 5 minutes. Transfer the fish to a baking sheet with the oil, and season with the thyme, fennel, lemon juice and salt and pepper to taste. Arrange the remaining garlic cloves, unpeeled, around the fish and push the bay leaf under the fish.
4. Cook in a preheated oven for about 20 minutes.
5. Serve with the roasted garlic, and grilled tomatoes, if liked.

ROUILLE

●

2 large garlic cloves, peeled and finely chopped
2 red chillies, chopped
stale bread, soaked in water and squeezed out to the size of a large walnut
2-3 tablespoons olive oil

Preparation time: 5 minutes

1. Grind the garlic to a paste in a pestle and mortar (the quantity is too small for a food processor). Pound in the chillies and nut of bread until smooth.
2. Whisk in the oil until the mixture becomes like a shining red mustard.

AIOLI

●

8 garlic cloves, peeled and crushed
2 egg yolks
450 ml (¾ pint) good olive oil
juice of 1 lemon
salt
freshly ground black pepper

Preparation time: 5-10 minutes

1. Whisk the garlic with the egg yolks, then dribble in the oil, whisking constantly, to make a thick, yellow mayonnaise. Stir in the lemon juice, and salt and pepper to taste.
2. Alternatively, make the mayonnaise in a food processor, still adding the oil very slowly.

STUFFED SQUID

Serves 4

●

4 medium-size squid, cleaned and skinned, and tentacles reserved
4 tablespoons olive oil
2 garlic cloves, peeled and bruised
400 g (14 oz) ripe tomatoes, chopped
150 ml (¼ pint) water
4 tablespoons dry white wine
½ teaspoon fresh rosemary
Stuffing:
3 tablespoons fresh breadcrumbs
2 tablespoons finely chopped fresh parsley
6 tablespoons grated Parmesan cheese
2 garlic cloves, peeled and chopped
1 egg, beaten
pinch of cayenne pepper
2 tablespoons olive oil
juice of 1 lemon
salt
freshly ground black pepper

Preparation time: 25 minutes
Cooking time: about 40 minutes

1. Finely chop the tentacles and mix with the stuffing ingredients. Use to stuff the squid bodies and sew up the ends with a needle and fine butcher's thread.
2. Heat the oil in a large pan and cook the garlic until it is browned and the oil is flavoured, then discard.
3. Add the squid to the oil and brown on all sides.
4. Meanwhile, put the tomatoes and water into a blender or food processor and blend until smooth. Strain off all skin and pips.
5. Add the tomato liquid to the pan with the wine and rosemary. Cover and simmer gently for about 30 minutes, turning the squid carefully from time to time.
6. Slice the squid crossways and serve with the sauce.

Top: Stuffed squid; bottom: Roast monkfish with garlic

46

BASS WITH SPRING ONION AND GINGER

Serves 4

•

1 bass, about 1 kg (2¼ lb),
gutted, cleaned and scaled
salt
juice of 1 lemon
Marinade:
1 tablespoon soy sauce
1 tablespoon cornflour
1 tablespoon rice wine or
dry sherry
¼ teaspoon ground ginger
freshly ground black
pepper
Sauce:
1 tablespoon chicken stock
2 tablespoons rice wine or
dry sherry
1 teaspoon sugar
½ tablespoon finely grated
fresh root ginger
2 leeks, white parts only,
very thinly sliced into rings
6 tablespoons bland oil
4 spring onions, quartered
lengthways

---

*Preparation time: 20 minutes
plus marinating
Cooking time: about 30 minutes*

---

1. Rub salt into the fish,
then bathe it in the lemon
juice for 10 minutes on each
side.
2. Rinse the fish and pat
dry. Cut some incisions
into the fish on both sides.
Put it in a shallow dish. Mix
together the ingredients for
the marinade and pour over
the fish. Leave to marinate
for 15-20 minutes, turning
it over several times.
3. Meanwhile, prepare the
sauce. Mix together the
stock, wine or sherry, sugar
and a pinch of salt and set

aside. Cook the ginger and
leeks gently in the oil for 10
minutes. Remove them
from the pan with a slotted
spoon and set aside.
4. Add the fish to the pan
and fry gently for 3 minutes
on each side. Add the
sherry mixture, the leek
and ginger mixture and the
spring onions, then cover
and cook gently for a
further 15 minutes.

WARM SEAFOOD SALAD

Serves 4

•

200 g (7 oz) carrots, peeled
and cut into matchsticks
(*julienne*)
200 g (7 oz) baby turnips,
peeled and cut into
matchsticks (*julienne*)
400 g (14 oz) fine green
beans
50 g (2 oz) butter
2 large onions, peeled and
chopped
3 garlic cloves, peeled and
chopped
150 ml (¼ pint) dry white
wine
1 tablespoon chopped fresh
parsley
40 fresh mussels, well
scrubbed
8 fresh scallops, removed
from shells
8 oysters, removed from
shells
juice of 1 lemon
5 tablespoons double cream
salt
freshly ground black
pepper
20 prawns or langoustines,
freshly cooked and peeled
1 tablespoon chopped
fresh parsley and chervil
4 puff pastry shapes

---

*Preparation time: 30 minutes
Cooking time: 45 minutes*

---

1. Cook the carrots, turnips and beans in separate
pans of boiling water until
just tender. Drain and allow
to cool completely.
2. Melt the butter in a large
pan, add the onions and
garlic and cook until
softened. Add the wine and
bring to the boil. Add the
parsley and mussels, cover
and cook, shaking the pan
from time to time, until the
mussels open (discard any
that remain closed). Re-
move the mussels, draining
the liquid from the shells
back into the pot. Remove
the mussels from their
shells and set aside.
3. Strain the mussel cooking liquid through a fine
sieve and return it to the
rinsed-out pan. Add the
scallops and simmer for 1½
minutes. Add the oysters
and simmer for a further
1½ minutes. Remove the
seafood with a slotted
spoon and set aside.
4. Boil the cooking liquid
until reduced to 150 ml (¼
pint). Add the lemon juice,
cream and salt and pepper
to taste and bring back to
the boil. Add the mussels,
scallops, oysters and
prawns or langoustines and
simmer for 2-3 minutes,
until they have warmed up
again.
5. Arrange the vegetables
attractively on white plates.
Add the warmed seafood
mixture and garnish with
herbs and pastry shapes.

*From the left; Bass with spring
onion and ginger; Warm seafood
salad*

DELIA SMITH

is famous for her enormously successful BBC series *Delia Smith's Cookery Course*, accompanied by a series of three books covering all aspects of cooking, as well as many other TV appearances and her long-running column in a London evening newspaper. She has a huge following among cookery enthusiasts and her books include *How To Cheat At Cooking*, *Delia Smith's Book of Cakes*, *Frugal Food* and *The Evening Standard Cookbook*. She is married to the writer Michael Wynn-Jones and writes a column for the *Radio Times*.

CHEESE SOUFFLE

Serves 3-4 people

The one and only secret of success in making a soufflé is to *whisk the egg whites* properly. Once you have mastered that, soufflés should never be a problem. But do remember it is in the nature of soufflés to start to shrink straight away, and always serve them absolutely immediately.

•

3 oz grated cheese (75 g) (any hard cheese can be used)
3 large eggs, separated
1 oz plain flour (25 g)
1 oz butter (25 g)
¼ pint milk (50 ml)
A pinch cayenne pepper
¼ teaspoon mustard powder
A little freshly-grated nutmeg
Salt and freshly-milled pepper
Pre-heat the oven to gas mark 5, 375°F (190°C)

For this you will need a 1½ pint (850 ml) soufflé dish or a pie-dish, butter it well.

First of all in a medium saucepan melt the butter, then add the flour and stir it over a moderate heat for 2 minutes.

Gradually add the milk to the saucepan – stirring all the time – and simmer gently for 3 minutes, still giving it an occasional stir. Then stir in the cayenne, mustard, nutmeg and a seasoning of salt and pepper, and leave the sauce to cool a little before stirring in the grated cheese. Beat the egg yolks thoroughly, then stir them in.

Next whisk the egg whites till they are stiff, take a couple of spoonfuls and beat them into the sauce, then fold in the rest very carefully. Transfer the mixture to the soufflé dish, place on a baking sheet in the centre of the oven and bake for 30-35 minutes. The soufflé is cooked when a skewer inserted into the centre comes out clean.

PEPPERED LIVER

Serves 2 people

This is more or less the same as *Steak au poivre* but quite a bit cheaper and – if you like liver – every bit as good.

•

12 oz lambs' liver (350 g) – ask the butcher to cut it into the thinnest slices possible
2 teaspoons whole black peppercorns
1 tablespoon flour
1 tablespoon olive oil
1 teaspoon butter
5 fl oz red (or white) wine (150 ml)
1 level teaspoon salt

You'll need to crush the peppercorns first, and this can present one or two problems. If you've got a pestle and mortar you're home and dry; if you haven't, then the best way to crush them is by exerting a lot of pressure on the back of a tablespoon with the peppercorns underneath it. This last method can often result in one or two peppercorns escaping and rolling off onto the floor, if you're not careful. So be warned.

When you've got the peppercorns coarsely crushed, add them to the flour with a level teaspoon of salt. Then dip the pieces of liver in it, pressing the pepper in a bit on both sides. Now in a large heavy-based frying pan, heat the oil and butter to the foamy stage, then put the liver slices in and cook them gently for a minute or two. As soon as the blood starts to run, turn them over, and gently cook them on the other side for slightly less time.

Whatever you do, don't overcook the liver or it will be dry and tough. Transfer the slices onto a warm serving dish, add the wine to the pan, let it bubble and reduce, then pour it over the liver and serve the wine immediately.

GRATIN DAUPHINOIS

Serves 3-4 people

This is one of the greatest potato dishes I've ever tasted. I know it does seem extravagant to use ¼ pint (150 ml) cream for 1 lb (450 g) potatoes, but I would forgo a pudding with cream once in a while in order to justify it.

•

1 lb good-quality potatoes (Edwards or Desirée) (450 g)
1½ oz butter (40 g)
¼ pint double cream (150 ml)
¼ pint milk (150 ml)
1 small clove garlic, crushed
Whole nutmeg
Salt and freshly-milled black pepper
Pre-heat the oven to gas mark 2, 300°F (150°C)
A *shallow* gratin dish well buttered

First, peel the potatoes and slice them very, very thinly (a wooden mandoline is excellent for this operation, if you have one), then plunge the potato slices into a bowl of cold water and swill them round and round to get rid of some of the starch. Now dry them very thoroughly in a clean teacloth. Then in the gratin dish arrange a layer of potato slices, a sprinkling of crushed garlic, pepper and salt and then another layer of potatoes and seasoning.

Now mix the cream and milk together, pour it over

DELIA SMITH AT HOME

50

the potatoes, sprinkle with a little freshly-grated whole nutmeg, then add the butter in flecks over the surface, and bake on the highest shelf in the oven for 1½ hours.

Note: Sometimes cheese is added to this, but I think it masks the potato flavour too much.

From the left: Cheese soufflé; Gratin dauphinois; Peppered liver

FOUR STAR SALAD

Serves 4 people

This salad is a meal in itself. The 'stars' in question here are avocado, garlic sausage, mushroom and lettuce with a lovely, garlicky, soured cream dressing.

•

2 ripe avocados
4 oz small pink-gilled mushrooms (110 g)
8 oz French garlic sausage, in one piece (225 g)
2 cloves garlic, crushed
1 tablespoon lemon juice
2 tablespoons mayonnaise
2 tablespoons olive oil
1 tablespoon wine vinegar
1 teaspoon mustard powder
1 medium-sized lettuce
4 spring onions, finely chopped
5 fl oz soured cream (150 ml)
Salt and freshly-milled black pepper

Begin by combining the soured cream with the garlic, mayonnaise and mustard powder. Then mix together the oil, vinegar and lemon juice and gradually add these to the soured cream mixture, tasting and seasoning with some salt and pepper. Now slice the garlic sausage into ½ inch (1 cm) slices and then cut these slices into ½ inch (1 cm) strips. Next break up the lettuce leaves and arrange them in a salad bowl: wipe and thinly slice the mushrooms (don't take the skins off) and add these to the lettuce pieces.

Finally prepare the avocados by removing the stones and peeling them, then cutting them into ½ inch (1 cm) cubes. Add these to the lettuce and mushrooms along with the strips of garlic sausage. Mix it all together gently, then add the dressing and toss again very gently. Sprinkle the chopped spring onions all over the surface and serve straightaway.

AMERICAN HAMBURGERS

Serves 2 people

In this country the word hamburger conjures up all sorts of dubious connotations of frozen and packaged discs of meat and greasy griddles. The real hamburger is something else: 100% pure ground beef cooked, if possible, over charcoal to give it a charred, smoky crispness at the edges with a juicy medium-rare centre. All it needs then is a jacket potato brimming with soured cream and chives, and a selection of relishes and

ketchup. This recipe will make 4 hamburgers to serve in buns, or two half-pounders (which may need a few more minutes cooking, depending on how you like them).

•

1 lb chuck steak, about 80% lean meat and 20% fat (450 g)
2 level teaspoons salt
Coarsely ground black pepper
A little oil

To prepare the meat you can either pass it through the fine blade of the mincer twice (which tenderises it), ask the butcher to do it for you, or you can grind the meat finely in a food processor.

To make the hamburgers, place the meat in a bowl and sprinkle in the salt and a good seasoning of coarsely ground black pepper.

Mix this in thoroughly, then divide the mixture into four portions. Take each portion in your hands and shape it into a ball, then place the ball on a flat surface and press to flatten it into a hamburger shape about ¾ inch (2 cm) thick.

Now brush each hamburger with very little oil and grill under a pre-heated grill set to high, or over hot charcoal, giving them 4-6 minutes on each side depending on how you like them. Serve in bap rolls (toasted on cut side only), and spread with slivers of raw or fried onion, relish and tomato ketchup.

Opposite, from left: Four star salad; American hamburgers.

RICH LEMON CREAM WITH FROSTED GRAPES

Serves 12 people

This is the very nicest lemon dessert I've ever come across. It serves about 12 people, so is very good for a party. For a smaller quantity, use a 6 inch (15 cm) tin, 1 level dessertspoon gelatine, 1 egg yolk and half the remaining ingredients.

•

5 fl oz milk (150 ml)
4 level tablespoons caster sugar
Grated rind and juice of 4 lemons
1 level tablespoon powdered gelatine
1 egg yolk
1¼ pints double cream (700 ml)
4 large egg whites

To decorate:
4 oz white grapes (110 g)
1 egg white
Caster sugar
An 8 inch (20 cm) round cake tin, lightly oiled

Place the milk, sugar, grated lemon rind, gelatine and egg yolk together in a blender or liquidiser. Blend for half a minute at top speed, then pour the mixture into a small saucepan, and stir over very gentle heat for 3 or 4 minutes until fairly hot but *not* boiling. Now return the mixture to the liquidiser and whizz round again, adding the lemon juice and ½ pint (275 ml) of the cream. When all is thoroughly blended, pour the mixture into a bowl, cover with foil and chill, stirring occasionally until the mixture is syrupy.

Whip the remaining cream lightly until it just begins to thicken, then in another very large bowl

whisk the egg whites until stiff and carefully fold them into the lemon mixture, followed by the cream. Pour the mixture into the cake tin, cover and chill until firm.

To make the frosted grapes: first of all whisk up the egg white. Then break the grapes into little clusters of 2 or 3 grapes each and dip each bunch first in the egg white, then in a saucer of caster sugar. Leave them spread out on greaseproof paper for a couple of hours before using them.

Before serving, dip the cake tin for a moment in hot water, and turn the lemon cream over onto a plate. Decorate with the frosted grapes and serve the cream cut in slices rather like a cake.

Below: Rich lemon cream with frosted grapes

DELIA SMITH AT HOME

53

PATRICK ANTHONY

MAGNIFICENT MUSHROOM SOUP

Serves 6-8
●

2 tablespoons oil
2 onions, peeled and
chopped
1 garlic clove, peeled and
crushed
450 g (1 lb) mushrooms,
sliced
2 tablespoons tomato purée
1.2 litres (2 pints) chicken
stock
50 g (2 oz) Parmesan
cheese, grated
2 tablespoons chopped
fresh parsley
5 egg yolks
1 glass of port

---

*Preparation time: 10 minutes
Cooking time: 45 minutes*

---

1. Heat the oil in a large saucepan and cook the onions and garlic until softened. Add the mushrooms and cook gently for a further 10 minutes, stirring frequently.
2. Blend the tomato purée with the stock and add to the pan. Bring to the boil and simmer gently for 15 minutes.
3. Mix together the Parmesan, parsley and egg yolks in a mixing bowl. Add a ladleful of the hot soup and beat well, then return this mixture to the pan. Add the port. Cook, stirring occasionally, for 5 minutes longer. Do not allow the Mushroom soup to boil or it will curdle.
4. Serve with toasted buttered slices of French bread or croûtons.

has enjoyed a wide-ranging career which spans journalism, theatre as an actor/producer and catering as a restaurateur as well as television as a popular cookery presenter. In 'Patrick's Pantry', his regular weekly item in the magazine programme *About Anglia* he has amused and instructed his one and a half million viewers. His relaxed style convinces viewers that they will be able to emulate his results in their own kitchens. Born in Dublin, he now lives in Norwich with his actress wife and two children.

CRAB GRATINE

Serves 2
●

1 medium crab, cooked
50 g (2 oz) fresh
breadcrumbs
100 g (4 oz) cheese, grated
¼ teaspoon powdered
mustard
½ teaspoon cayenne
pepper
few drops of
Worcestershire sauce
salt
freshly ground black
pepper
about 3 tablespoons cream
2 bananas, peeled and
sliced
15 g (½ oz) butter
watercress, to garnish

---

*Preparation time: 30 minutes
Cooking time: 20 minutes
Oven: 200°C, 400°F,
Gas Mark 6*

---

1. To prepare the crab, lay it on its back and, holding the shell firmly with one hand and the body (to which the claws are attached) with the other, pull apart. Using a spoon, remove the stomach bag (which lies below the head) and the greyish white frond-like pieces (dead man's fingers) from the shell and discard. Care-

fully scrape all the meat from the shell into a bowl and reserve.
2. Wash and, if necessary, scrub the shell, then dry and polish. Knock away the edge as far as the dark line. Set the shell aside.
3. Remove the meat from the claws, except the tiny ones. Add the meat to the bowl. Reserve the tiny claws for the garnish.
4. Mix the dark and white crabmeat with the breadcrumbs, cheese, mustard, cayenne pepper, Worcestershire sauce, and salt and pepper to taste. Add enough cream to bind to a fairly soft consistency.
5. Pack the crab mixture into the shell. Bake in a preheated oven for 20 minutes.
6. Just before the crab is ready, fry the banana slices in the butter until lightly browned.
7. Serve the crab on a bed of watercress, garnished with the tiny claws and fried banana slices.

From the top: Magnificent mushroom soup: Smoked haddock mousse; Crab gratiné

SMOKED HADDOCK MOUSSE

Serves 6-8
●

450 g (1 lb) smoked
haddock fillet
120 ml (4 fl oz) milk
2 hard boiled eggs
50 g (2 oz) softened butter
½ teaspoon nutmeg
½ teaspoon mace
½ teaspoon cayenne
pepper
salt
freshly ground white
pepper

---

*Preparation time: 20 minutes,
plus setting overnight
Cooking time: 15 minutes*

---

1. Remove the skin and bones from the fish and cut it into small pieces (2.5 cm/1 inch cubes).
2. Place the fish and milk in a pan, cover and poach the fish for 5 minutes. Remove the fish with a slotted spoon and put in a blender or food processor.
3. Add the eggs, butter, ⅜ of the poaching milk, nutmeg, mace and cayenne pepper. Add salt and pepper. Blend until very smooth.
4. Place in 2 small pots, cover with clingfilm and allow to set in the refrigerator overnight.
5. Remove from the refrigerator, dip into hot water for 5 seconds and invert on to serving dishes. Serve in very small portions with hot toast fingers and lemon wedges. Spread the mousse on toast and add lemon juice to taste.

BEAUJOLAIS BEEF

Serves 4

●

500 g (1¼ lb) top rump of
beef, cubed
1 tablespoon flour seasoned
with salt and pepper
2 tablespoons oil
25 g (1 oz) butter
2 onions, peeled and sliced
1 garlic clove, peeled and
crushed
225 g (8 oz) stoned prunes
½ teaspoon ground
cinnamon
½ teaspoon mixed spice
300 ml (½ pint) Beaujolais
or other fruity red wine
300 ml (½ pint) beef stock
1 tablespoon tomato purée

Preparation time: 10 minutes
Cooking time: 2 hours
Oven: 180°C, 350°F,
Gas Mark 4

1. Dust the meat with the
seasoned flour. Heat the oil
in a frying pan and brown
the cubes of meat on all
sides.
2. In another pan, melt the
butter and cook the onions
and garlic gently until they
have softened.
3. Combine the meat and
onion mixture in a cas-
serole and add the prunes
and spices. Blend the wine,
stock and tomato purée and
add to the casserole. Stir to
distribute evenly.
4. Cover the casserole and
cook in a preheated oven for
about 1½ hours or until the
meat is tender. Add addi-
tional stock or wine during
cooking if this becomes
necessary.
5. Serve with boiled rice or
creamed potatoes.

LIVER AND APPLE BAKE

PATRICK ANTHONY AT HOME

Serves 4

•

1 onion, peeled and sliced
1 cooking apple, peeled,
cored and sliced
225 g (8 oz) liver, sliced
salt
freshly ground black
pepper
250 ml (8 fl oz) tomato juice
100 g (4 oz) tomatoes, sliced

Preparation time: 20 minutes
Cooking time: 55-65 minutes
Oven: 200°C, 400°F,
Gas Mark 6

---

1. Scatter the onion and half the apple over the bottom of a casserole dish. Arrange the liver slices on top and cover with the remaining apple. Add salt and pepper to taste. Pour over the tomato juice.
2. Cover and cook in a pre-heated oven for about 50-60 minutes, depending on the thickness of the liver slices.
3. Remove the lid. Arrange the tomato slices over the liver. Bake for a further 5 minutes.
4. Serve on a bed of hot boiled rice.

From the left: Beaujolais beef; Liver and apple bake

57

Lamb with Lemon Sauce
Serves 4-6

●

2 tablespoons oil
750 g (1½ lb) lean boneless
lamb, cubed
50 g (2 oz) butter
1 onion, peeled and finely
chopped
2 garlic cloves, peeled and
crushed
175 ml (6 fl oz) dry white
wine
120 ml (4 fl oz) chicken
stock
2 teaspoons chopped fresh
sage
salt
freshly ground black
pepper
grated rind of 1 lemon
juice of 2 lemons
2 egg yolks
chopped fresh parsley

*Preparation time: 10 minutes
Cooking time: 1½ hours*

1. Heat the oil in a flame-proof casserole and brown the lamb cubes on all sides. Remove and set aside.
2. Add the butter to the casserole, then cook the onion and garlic until softened.
3. Stir in the wine, stock, sage, and salt and pepper to taste. Bring to the boil. Return the lamb cubes to the casserole and cover. Simmer gently for 1 hour or until the meat is tender.
4. Beat together the lemon rind and juice and egg yolks. Add about 3 tablespoons of the hot liquid from the casserole, then stir this mixture into the casserole. Cook gently for about 1 minute, stirring. Do not allow to boil. Serve sprinkled with parsley.

58

ANTHONY'S AUBERGINES

Serves 4

●

2 good-sized aubergines
oil for deep frying
275 g (10 oz) minced lamb,
beef or sausagemeat
1 garlic clove, crushed
salt
freshly ground black
pepper
3 tablespoons fresh
breadcrumbs
1 tablespoon grated
Parmesan cheese (optional)
1 tablespoon chopped fresh
parsley
25-50 g (1-2 oz) butter, cut
into small pieces

Preparation time: 20 minutes
Cooking time: 35 minutes
Oven: 180°C, 350°F,
Gas Mark 4

---

1. Cut the aubergines in half lengthways and score the flesh with a sharp knife, taking care not to break the skin. Deep fry for 2-3 minutes, then drain well on paper towels.
2. Scoop out the aubergine pulp and chop it finely. Set the aubergine shells aside.
3. Mix the chopped aubergine pulp with the meat, garlic, salt and pepper. Use to fill the shells.
4. Arrange the stuffed shells in an oiled baking dish. Mix together the breadcrumbs, Parmesan, if using, and parsley and sprinkle over the tops of the shells. Dot with the butter.
5. Bake in a preheated oven for 30 minutes. Serve hot.

From the left: Lamb with lemon sauce; Anthony's aubergines

PATRICK ANTHONY AT HOME

59

MARY BERRY

DUTCH PEA SOUP

Serves 6-8

●

450 g (1 lb) green split peas
450 g (1 lb) gammon
knuckle, or 2 pig's trotters
2.25 litres (4 pints) water
225 g (8 oz) onions, peeled
and chopped
4 celery stalks, chopped
4 potatoes, peeled and
diced
2 leeks, sliced
1 tablespoon chopped fresh
parsley
salt
freshly ground black
pepper
25 g (1 oz) unsalted butter

---

*Preparation time: 15 minutes
plus soaking
Cooking time: 3¾ hours*

---

1. Soak the peas and
knuckle or trotters in cold
water to cover overnight.
2. Drain the peas and
knuckle or trotters and
place them in a pan with the
water. Bring to the boil and
simmer for 1 hour.
3. Add the onions, celery
and potatoes. Cover and
simmer for 2½ hours.
4. Remove the knuckle or
trotters from the pan and
remove the meat from the
bones. Return the meat to
the soup.
5. Add the leeks, parsley
and salt and pepper to
taste. Stir in the butter.
Bring back to the boil, and
serve hot.

is well-known to millions of afternoon viewers
through her long-running cookery spot on Thames
television's magazine programme *After Noon Plus*. Her
enormous range of recipes appeals to everyone from
the novice to the most experienced cook and she is a
best-selling writer too, with over 20 cookery books to
her credit. She was born in Bath and studied cookery
there and in Paris before becoming cookery editor of
Ideal Home and later cookery consultant for *Home and
Freezer Digest*.

CELEBRATION TURKEY MAYONNAISE

Serves 6

●

1 small onion, peeled and
chopped
½ garlic clove, peeled
1 tablespoon tomato purée
½ teaspoon curry powder
2 tablespoons lemon juice
2 tablespoons apricot jam
150-300 ml (¼-½ pint)
mayonnaise
350-450 g (12 oz-1 lb)
cooked turkey meat,
chopped
225 g (8 oz) green and black
grapes, halved and pipped
40 g (1½ oz) toasted flaked
almonds
small watercress or parsley
sprigs, to garnish

---

*Preparation time: 20 minutes
plus chilling
Cooking time: 5 minutes*

---

1. Put the onion, garlic,
tomato purée, curry
powder, 1 tablespoon
lemon juice and the apricot
jam in a small saucepan and
slowly bring to the boil,
stirring constantly. Allow
the mixture to cool slightly,
then purée it in a blender or
food processor until
smooth.

2. Mix the puréed mixture
with the mayonnaise, then
fold in the turkey. Chill
overnight.
3. Toss the grapes in the
remaining lemon juice and
fold into the turkey mayonnaise.
4. Pile into a serving dish
and sprinkle with the al-
monds. Garnish with sprigs
of watercress or parsley.

*From the left: Dutch pea soup;
Celebration turkey mayonnaise*

BEEF PARCELS

Serves 4

●

4 slices beef silverside
Stuffing:
25 g (1 oz) butter
50 g (2 oz) bacon, rinded
and chopped
50 g (2 oz) mushrooms,
chopped
50 g (2 oz) fresh white
breadcrumbs
1 tablespoon chopped fresh
parsley
salt
freshly ground black
pepper
Sauce:
25 g (1 oz) dripping
25 g (1 oz) plain flour
300 ml (½ pint) beef stock
2 tablespoons sherry
6 celery stalks, sliced

Preparation time: 25 minutes
Cooking time: 2-2½ hours

1. Trim the meat, then place each piece in turn between sheets of wetted greaseproof paper and beat flat with a rolling pin.
2. To prepare the stuffing, melt the butter in a small pan and fry the bacon and mushrooms gently for 2-3 minutes. Stir in the remaining stuffing ingredients.
3. Divide the stuffing into four portions and place one on each slice of meat. Roll up and tie with fine string, or secure with wooden cocktail sticks.
4. Melt the dripping in a large saucepan and brown the beef rolls on all side. Remove from the pan and set aside.
5. Stir the flour into the fat in the pan and cook for 2 minutes. Add the stock and sherry and bring to the boil,

stirring until thickened. Add the celery and salt and pepper to taste.
6. Return the beef rolls to the sauce. Cover tightly and

simmer gently for 1½-2 hours or until tender.
7. Remove the string or cocktail sticks before serving.

From the left: Beef parcels; Lamb boulangère

62

LAMB BOULANGERE

Serves 6-8

●

1 small leg of lamb
2 cloves garlic, peeled and
cut into slivers
sprig of fresh rosemary
750 g ($1\frac{1}{2}$ lb) potatoes,
peeled and sliced
225 g (8 oz) onions, peeled
and sliced
salt
freshly ground black
pepper
300 ml ($\frac{1}{2}$ pint) stock
a little chopped parsley

---

*Preparation time: 25 minutes
Cooking time: 30 minutes per
pound, plus 30 minutes over
Oven: 190°C, 375°F,
Gas Mark 5*

Delicious with casseroled carrots cooked in the oven in butter and stock.

1. Trim any excess fat from the lamb and then insert the garlic into the lamb. Tie the sprig of rosemary over the lamb.

2. Mix the onions with the potatoes and lay them in a shallow ovenproof dish and season well. Place the lamb on top and pour over the stock.

3. Cover with a piece of foil and roast in the preheated oven. After the first hour, remove the foil, baste the meat and vegetables and cook until tender.

4. When cooked, untie the rosemary and lay a fresh sprig in its place. Sprinkle the vegetables with a little chopped parsley.

MARY BERRY AT HOME

63

CARAMEL CUSTARD

Serves 4

•

Caramel:
75 g (3 oz) granulated sugar
3 tablespoons water
Custard:
4 eggs
40 g (1½ oz) caster sugar
few drops of vanilla essence
600 ml (1 pint) milk

---

*Preparation time: 10 minutes
plus chilling
Cooking time: 1 hour 35-40
minutes
Oven: 150°C, 300°F,
Gas Mark 2*

---

1. To make the caramel, put the sugar and water in a heavy saucepan and bring to the boil, stirring to dissolve the sugar. Boil until the syrup is a pale golden brown.
2. Quickly pour the syrup into a 900 ml (1½ pint) charlotte mould or soufflé dish and tilt to cover the bottom evenly. Set aside.
3. For the custard, mix together the eggs, sugar and vanilla essence. Warm the milk until it is hand-hot, then stir it into the egg mixture.
4. Butter the sides of the mould or dish above the layer of caramel. Strain the custard into the mould. Place the mould in a tin of hot water.
5. Bake in a preheated oven for 1½ hours or until a knife inserted into the centre of the custard comes out clean.
6. Remove from the tin of water and allow the custard to cool completely, for at least 12 hours or overnight in the refrigerator.
7. When ready to serve, turn out onto a flat serving dish.

LEMON MERINGUE PIE

Serves 6

•

Pastry:
175 g (6 oz) plain flour
50 g (2 oz) butter
50 g (2 oz) lard
1 egg yolk
1 tablespoon caster sugar
2 teaspoons cold water
Filling:
finely grated rind and juice
of 2 large lemons
40 g (1½ oz) cornflour
300 ml (½ pint) water
2 egg yolks
75 g (3 oz) caster sugar
Meringue topping:
3 egg whites
120 g (4½ oz) caster sugar

---

*Preparation time: 30 minutes
plus chilling
Cooking time: 45 minutes
Oven: 220°C, 425°F,
Gas Mark 7; then
160°C, 325°F,
Gas Mark 3*

---

1. First make the pastry. Put the flour into a bowl and rub in the fats until the mixture resembles breadcrumbs. Mix the egg yolk, sugar and water together and add to the dry ingredients. Mix to a dough.
2. Roll out the dough and use to line a 23 cm (9 inch) flan tin. Chill for 30 minutes.
3. Line the pastry case with greaseproof paper and weight down with baking beans. Bake blind in a preheated oven for 15 minutes.
4. Meanwhile, prepare the filling. Mix together the lemon rind and juice, cornflour and 2 tablespoons of the water. Bring the remaining water to the boil and pour it onto the cornflour mixture, stirring well. Return to the pan and bring back to the boil, stirring constantly. Remove from the heat and add the egg yolks and sugar. Stir well. Return to the heat for a moment to thicken the sauce, but do not allow to boil. Leave to cool slightly.
5. Remove the beans and paper from the pastry case, and pour in the filling.
6. For the topping, whisk the egg whites until stiff, then gradually whisk in the sugar. Spoon the meringue over the filling, sealing it to the pastry and leaving no air spaces.
7. Reduce the oven temperature and bake for about 30 minutes or until the meringue is golden brown.

APRICOT AND ORANGE MARMALADE

Makes 4.5 kg (10 lb)

•

750 g (1½ lb) Seville
oranges
1 lemon
450 g (1 lb) dried apricots
3 litres (5½ pints) water
2.75 kg (6 lb) sugar

---

*Preparation time: 30 minutes
plus soaking and cooling
Cooking time: about 1 hour*

---

1. Scrub the oranges and lemon, then cut them in half and squeeze out the juice into a large bowl. Scrape the pith from the skins with a teaspoon and put it with the seeds in a smaller bowl. Shred the skins finely and put in the bowl with the juice.
2. Halve or quarter the apricots and add to the bowl with the juice. Add 2.5 litres (4½ pints) of the water. Pour the remaining water over the pith and seeds. Cover both bowls and leave to soak for 24-36 hours.
3. Put the pith and seeds in a piece of muslin and tie with string to form a bag. Tie this bag to the handle of a large saucepan.
4. Pour the soaking water from the pith and seeds into the pan. Add the fruit mixture from the large bowl. Bring to the boil and simmer for about 45 minutes or until tender and the contents of the pan has reduced by about one-third.
5. Remove the muslin bag. Add the sugar to the pan and stir until it has dissolved. Boil rapidly until setting point is reached.
6. Remove from the heat and leave to cool for 20 minutes, then skim any scum from the surface and pot the marmalade into clean warm jars. Cover and label.

HOT CROSS BUNS

Makes 12

●

300 ml ($\frac{1}{2}$ pint) hand-hot milk
50 g (2 oz) plus 1 teaspoon caster sugar
15 g ($\frac{1}{2}$ oz) dried yeast
450 g (1 lb) strong bread flour
1 teaspoon salt
pinch of mixed spice
pinch of ground cinnamon
pinch of grated nutmeg
100 g (4 oz) currants
25 g (1 oz) chopped mixed candied peel
1 egg, beaten
25 g (1 oz) butter, melted
shortcrust pastry trimmings
Glaze:
2 tablespoons water
2 tablespoons milk
40 g ($1\frac{1}{2}$ oz) caster sugar

Preparation time: 40 minutes plus rising
Cooking time: 15-12 minutes
Oven: 220°C, 425°F, Gas Mark 7

---

1. Lightly whisk together the milk, 1 teaspoon sugar and yeast. Leave for 5-10 minutes or until frothy.
2. Sift the flour, salt and spices into a large bowl. Add the remaining sugar, currants and peel. Stir the egg and butter into the yeast mixture, then add to the bowl and mix well to a soft dough.
3. Turn out the dough onto a floured surface and knead for about 10 minutes or until smooth and no longer sticky. Place in a lightly oiled polythene bag and leave to rise at room tem-

perature for $1\frac{1}{2}$-2 hours or until doubled in bulk.
4. Punch down the dough, then divide into 12 pieces. Shape each into a bun and place, spaced well apart, on a floured baking sheet. Put inside the oiled polythene bag and leave to rise at room temperature for about 1 hour, or until doubled in bulk.

5. Remove the bag. Roll out the pastry trimmings and cut into 24 strips about 10 cm (4 inches) long and 5 mm ($\frac{1}{4}$ inch) wide. Place two strips in a cross on each bun, dampening the underside with water to make them stick.
6. Bake in a preheated oven for 15-20 minutes or until golden brown.

7. To make the glaze, bring the water and milk to the boil, then stir in the sugar and boil for 2 minutes.
8. Remove the buns from the oven and glaze at once. Cool on a wire rack.

Clockwise from top left: Apricot and orange marmalade; Hot cross buns; Caramel custard; Lemon meringue pie

MARGARET LAMB

is a leading authority on traditional Cumbrian fare and has shared her recipes with viewers of Border TV's *Country Kitchen* series and the BBC's *Look North*. After training in Bath and teaching home economics, she became head of the Rural Home Economics Department at the Cumbria College of Agriculture and Forestry in 1979. With her husband, she now runs Grizedale Lodge Hotel near Hawkshead in the Lake District, where she is making a speciality of traditional British cooking.

PENRITH PEPPERED LAMB

Serves 4

•

25 g (1 oz) butter
1 onion, peeled and chopped
450 g (1 lb) lean boneless lamb, cubed
40 g (1½ oz) plain flour
1 tablespoon vegetable oil
600 ml (1 pint) chicken stock
1 tablespoon tomato purée
4 teaspoons clear honey
1 teaspoon crumbled dried rosemary
salt
2 cooking apples, peeled, cored and cut into 1 cm (½ inch) cubes
Spiced pepper:
25 g (1 oz) white pepper
25 g (1 oz) grated nutmeg
25 g (1 oz) ground mace
15 g (½ oz) cayenne pepper

Preparation time: 15 minutes
Cooking time: about 2 hours
Oven: 170°C, 325°F, Gas Mark 3

---

1. Mix together all the ingredients for the spiced pepper thoroughly and store in an airtight jar until needed.
2. Melt the butter in a frying pan, add the onion and cook until softened but not brown. Add 1 teaspoon of the spiced pepper and cook, stirring, for a further 30 seconds.
3. Remove the onion from the pan with a slotted spoon and place in a casserole.
4. Toss the lamb cubes in the flour. Heat the oil with the butter in the frying pan, then add the lamb cubes and brown on all sides. Add

the stock, tomato purée, honey, rosemary and salt to taste. Stir well to mix.
5. Pour the lamb mixture into the casserole and mix with the onion. Cover and cook in a preheated oven for 1 hour.
6. Add the apples and stir well, then cover again and cook for a further 30 minutes.

CUMBERLAND SAUSAGE PIE

Serves 4-6

•

350 g (12 oz) strong bread flour
½ teaspoon salt
225 g (8 oz) hard margarine or butter, well chilled
about 6 tablespoons iced water
squeeze of lemon juice or few drops of vinegar
milk, to glaze
Filling:
450 g (1 lb) pork sausagemeat
2 bacon rashers, rinded and diced
good pinch of dried sage
good pinch of dried lemon thyme
1 tablespoon chopped fresh parsley
pinch of grated nutmeg
freshly ground black pepper
4 eggs

Preparation time: 30 minutes plus chilling
Cooking time: 40 minutes
Oven: 220°C, 425°F, Gas Mark 7;
then 170°C, 325°F, Gas Mark 3

---

1. Sift the flour and salt into a bowl. Grate in the fat, flouring the grater to prevent the fat from sticking. Mix the water with the lemon juice or vinegar and use to bind the flour mixture to a soft but not wet dough. Try not to break up the fat at this stage.
2. Turn onto a floured surface, shape into a rectangle and roll out to an oblong that is 3 times longer than its width. Fold up envelope style and turn so a folded edge is to the right. Repeat the rolling and folding once more, then wrap the dough and chill for 1 hour.
3. To make the filling, heat a frying pan, add the sausagemeat, bacon, herbs, nutmeg and pepper to taste and brown quickly, stirring to mix well. It is not necessary to cook the mixture through. Cool slightly.
4. Roll out two-thirds of the dough and use to line a 20 cm (8 inch) flan ring on a baking sheet, leaving the excess dough hanging over the sides of the ring.

5. Spread the filling in the pastry case and make 4 hollows in it. Drop an egg into each hollow and season with salt and pepper.

6. Roll out the remaining dough and use to cover the pie, sealing the edges well with a little water. Decorate the top with the dough trimmings, make a slit in the top and brush with milk.

7. Bake in a preheated oven for 15 minutes, then reduce the oven temperature and bake for a further 15 minutes or until the pastry is golden. Serve the pie hot or cold.

From the left: Penrith peppered lamb; Cumberland sausage pie

67

TASTY VENISON ROLL

Serves 6-8

•

1 kg (2 lb) boneless venison
450 g (1 lb) fat bacon
225 g (8 oz) fresh brown
breadcrumbs
½ tablespoon chopped
fresh marjoram
1 tablespoon chopped fresh
parsley
1 teaspoon salt
½ teaspoon freshly ground
black pepper
2 eggs, beaten
2 teaspoons Worcestershire
sauce
1 tablespoon tomato
ketchup
Spicy damson sauce:
350 g (12 oz) damsons,
halved and stoned
150 ml (¼ pint) port or
elderberry wine
pinch of ground cloves
good pinch of ground
cinnamon
25 g (1 oz) soft brown
sugar
3 tablespoons redcurrant
jelly
juice of ½ lemon
grated rind and juice of 1
orange
25 g (1 oz) butter

Preparation time: 20 minutes
Cooking time: 2 hours

1. Mince the venison and bacon together finely, or grind in a food processor. Tip into a bowl and add the breadcrumbs, herbs, salt, pepper, eggs, Worcestershire sauce and ketchup. Mix together well.
2. Shape the mixture into a roll and wrap tightly in a floured pudding cloth. Place in a wide pan of boil-

ing water and simmer gently for 2 hours.
3. Meanwhile, make the sauce. Put the damsons and wine in a saucepan and add the cloves, cinnamon and sugar. Bring to the boil, then cover and simmer for 15 minutes.
4. Add the redcurrant jelly, lemon juice, and orange rind and juice and stir to mix. Bring back to the boil.
5. Allow the sauce to cool slightly, then sieve it and return to the pan. Add the butter and pepper to taste.
6. Just before serving, reheat the sauce to serve with the venison roll.
7. The venison roll may also be served cold: drain it and tighten the cloth, then weight down slightly and leave to cool. Serve with redcurrant or rowan jelly.

RAISED PORK AND PINEAPPLE PIE

Serves 6-8

•

700 g (1½ lb) plain flour
2 teaspoons salt
175 g (6 oz) lard
150 ml (¼ pint) milk
300 ml (½ pint) water
beaten egg, to glaze
Filling:
700 g (1½ lb) pork
sausagemeat
1 × 450 g (15 oz) can
pineapple chunks, drained
50 g (2 oz) walnuts,
chopped
1 teaspoon dried sage
1 egg, beaten
salt
freshly ground black
pepper
450 g (1 lb) pork fillet, cut
into thin strips

Preparation time: 30 minutes
Cooking time: 1¾ hours
Oven: 190°C, 375°F,
Gas Mark 5;
then 180°C, 350°F,
Gas Mark 4

1. Sift the flour and salt into a bowl and rub in the lard until the mixture resembles breadcrumbs.

2. Bring the milk and water to the boil in a small saucepan. Add to the flour mixture and stir to make a smooth, firm dough.
3. Roll out two-thirds of the dough and use to line a 23 cm (9 inch) loose-bottomed non-stick round cake tin or raised pie mould. Wrap the remaining dough in a warm cloth and set aside.

OATMEAL ROLLS

Makes 16
•
225 g (8 oz) medium
oatmeal
300 ml (½ pint) milk
15 g (½ oz) fresh yeast
2 tablespoons tepid water
50 g (2 oz) margarine,
melted
1 teaspoon salt
225 g (8 oz) strong bread
flour
beaten egg, to glaze

*Preparation time: 25 minutes
plus soaking and rising
Cooking time: 20 minutes
Oven: 220°C, 425°F,
Gas Mark 7*

1. Put the oats and milk in a bowl and soak for at least 2 hours, or overnight.
2. Cream the yeast with the water, then add to the oats with the margarine, salt and enough flour to make a smooth dough. Knead on a floured surface for 10 minutes.
3. Put the dough into a lightly oiled polythene bag and leave to rise in a warm place for about 1 hour.
4. Knock back the dough and knead again until smooth. Divide into 16 equal portions and shape each into a bun. Cut a cross on the top of each bun.
5. Arrange the buns on a greased baking sheet, cover with the oiled polythene bag and leave in a warm place to prove until doubled in size.
6. Brush the buns with egg, then bake in a preheated oven for about 20 minutes. Cool on a wire rack.

MARGARET LAMB ■■■ AT HOME

4. Mix together the sausagemeat, pineapple, walnuts, sage, egg, and salt and pepper to taste.
5. Pack half the filling in the lined tin, then cover with the strips of pork. Spread the remaining filling on top.
6. Roll out the remaining dough and use to cover the pie, sealing the edges with beaten egg. Glaze the top with beaten egg.

7. Bake in a preheated oven for 1 hour, then reduce the oven temperature and bake for a further 45 minutes.
8. Allow to cool before removing from the tin or mould. Serve cold.

From the left: Tasty venison roll; Raised pork and pineapple pie; Oatmeal rolls

MANX BUN LOAF

Makes a 1 kg (2 lb) loaf

•

225 g (8 oz) plain flour
¼ teaspoon salt
2 teaspoons mixed spice
225 g (8 oz) currants
100 g (4 oz) sultanas
100 g (4 oz) seedless raisins
150 g (5 oz) soft brown
sugar
50 g (2 oz) chopped mixed
candied peel
1 medium cooking apple,
peeled, cored and coarsely
grated
50 g (2 oz) lard
1 tablespoon treacle
1 egg, beaten
1 teaspoon bicarbonate of
soda
150 ml (¼ pint) buttermilk

Preparation time: 20 minutes
Cooking time: 2 hours
Oven: 170°C, 325°F,
Gas Mark 3

1. Mix together the flour, salt, spice, currants, sultanas, raisins, sugar, peel and grated apple in a mixing bowl.
2. Warm the lard with the treacle until melted but not hot. Add to the fruit mixture with the egg and beat in well.
3. Dissolve the bicarbonate of soda in the buttermilk and stir until frothy, then add to the mixture and stir in.
4. Turn into a greased and lined 1 kg (2 lb) loaf tin. Bake in a preheated oven

for 2 hours. Cool in the tin.
5. If possible, store the loaf in an airtight tin for 2-3 days before serving, sliced and buttered.

HARLEQUIN FRUIT MERINGUE

Serves 6

•

3 egg whites
175 g (6 oz) caster sugar
25 g (1 oz) plain chocolate
150 ml (¼ pint) double or
whipping cream
100 g (4 oz) kiwi fruit,
peeled and sliced
100 g (4 oz) black grapes,
halved and pipped
100 g (4 oz) satsumas or
clementines, peeled and
segmented
100 g (4 oz) raspberries
100 g (4 oz) peeled fresh
pineapple, cut into chunks
100 g (4 oz) strawberries or
stoned cherries

Preparation time: 35-40 minutes
Cooking time: 3 hours
Oven: 110°C, 225°F,
Gas Mark ¼

1. Line a baking sheet with non-stick silicone paper and draw an 18.5 cm (7½ inch) circle on the paper.
2. Whisk the egg whites until stiff and dry. Gradually whisk in half the sugar, 1 teaspoon at a time, then fold in the remaining sugar with a metal spoon.
3. Fit a large piping bag with a fluted vegetable nozzle and fill with almost all the meringue. Spread the remaining meringue inside the circle drawn on the paper to make a round.
4. With a knife, lightly mark the meringue round into six equal wedges. Pipe a petal shape in each wedge to form six individual cases on top of the meringue round.
5. Bake in a preheated oven for 3 hours or until crisp and dry.
6. Remove the meringue from the baking sheet and carefully peel off the lining paper. Return the meringue to the baking sheet, upside down, and leave to dry out completely in the oven as it cools down.
7. Melt the chocolate and brush over the inside of each meringue case. Leave to set.
8. Whip the cream until thick and divide between the meringue cases. Fill each case with a different fruit. Serve immediately.

CUMBERLAND RUM NICKY

Serves 6
●
175 g (6 oz) plain flour
pinch of salt
90 g (3½ oz) butter
1 tablespoon caster sugar
1 egg yolk
little water to mix
Filling:
50 g (2 oz) butter
25 g (1 oz) soft brown sugar
2 tablespoons rum
100 g (4 oz) stoned dates, chopped
25 g (1 oz) stem or crystallized ginger, chopped
Glaze:
egg white
1½ teaspoons caster sugar

Preparation time: 20 minutes
plus chilling
Cooking time: 30-45 minutes
Oven: 190°C, 375°F,
Gas Mark 5

1. Sift the flour and salt into a bowl and rub in the butter until the mixture resembles breadcrumbs. Add the sugar, and bind with the egg yolk and a little water to make a smooth dough. Chill for 15-20 minutes.
2. Meanwhile, cream the butter with the sugar until light and fluffy, then beat in the rum.
3. Roll out two-thirds of the dough and use to line a 20 cm (8 inch) fluted flan ring on a baking sheet or a quiche dish. Sprinkle the dates and ginger over the bottom of the pastry case and cover with the rum butter mixture.
4. Roll out the remaining dough and cut into neat 5 mm (¼ inch) wide strips. Arrange over the top of the filling to make a lattice, interwoven if possible.
5. Brush the strips with egg white and sprinkle with the caster sugar. Bake in a preheated oven for 30-45 minutes.

MARGARET LAMB AT HOME

From the left: Manx bun loaf; Harlequin fruit meringue; Cumberland rum nicky

71

EVELYN ROSE

ONION SOUP GRATINEE

Serves 6

●

25 g (1 oz) butter
2 teaspoons oil
450 g (1 lb) onions, peeled
and thinly sliced
1 teaspoon sugar
salt
freshly ground black
pepper
25 g (1 oz) plain flour
1.8 litres (3 pints) hot beef
stock
120 ml (4 fl oz) dry white
wine or vermouth
6 slices French bread
grated cheese
1 tablespoon butter, melted

Preparation time: 15 minutes
Cooking time: about 1½ hours

---

1. Heat the butter with the oil in a heavy saucepan, add the onions and turn to coat with the fat. Cover and cook gently for 15 minutes.
2. Uncover and add the sugar and salt and pepper to taste. Cook, stirring occasionally, for about 3 minutes longer or until the onions are a rich golden brown.
3. Sprinkle in the flour and stir well, then cook for a further 3 minutes. Stir in the stock and wine or vermouth and bring to the boil. Half cover the pan and simmer for 1 hour.
4. Ladle the soup into deep heatproof serving bowls. Float a slice of bread in each and sprinkle with cheese. Drizzle over the melted butter. Cook under a preheated grill until the cheese has melted and is golden brown. Serve immediately.

first began cooking for the television cameras over 25 years ago; she is a frequent contributor to national and local radio and consultant to several leading food groups. She is the author of classic books on Jewish cookery, *New Jewish Cuisine* and *The Complete International Jewish Cookbook*, and past National Chairman of the Institute of Home Economics. She has always been deeply concerned with consumer affairs and is a member of two national consumer committees. She holds regular master classes in food and wine.

FISHERMAN'S CASSEROLE

Serves 4-6

●

750 g (1½ lb) white fish
fillets
50 g (2 oz) butter
½ large carrot, grated
½ onion, peeled and grated
salt
white pepper
1 small bay leaf
10 black peppercorns
2 teaspoons cornflour
1 small can (175 g/6 oz)
evaporated milk, or 150 ml
(¼ pint) single cream
1 × 850 g (29 oz) can new
potatoes, drained
1 small packet frozen peas,
cooked (optional)
chopped fresh parsley, to
garnish

Preparation time: 10 minutes
Cooking time: 35 minutes

---

1. Cut thick fillets of fish into 4-6 pieces; roll up thinner fillets.
2. Melt the butter in a 23 cm (9 inch) pan and add the carrot and onion. Cook, stirring, for 1-2 minutes, then add the fish and turn it over to coat with the buttery vegetables. Add water to cover the bottom of the pan to a depth of 5 mm (¼ inch). Add salt and pepper

to taste, then tuck the bay leaf and peppercorns, at the side of the pan.
3. Cover and simmer very gently for 20 minutes or until the fish looks creamy right through.
4. Remove the bay leaf and peppercorns. Blend the cornflour with the evaporated milk or cream and add to the pan. Cook, stirring, until thickened.
5. Add the potatoes and peas, if used. Cover and cook very gently for 3-4 minutes to heat through the vegetables.
6. Serve sprinkled with parsley.

CUMBERLAND CUTLETS

Serves 4-5

●

6-8 lamb cutlets, trimmed
of excess fat
salt
freshly ground black
pepper
1 egg, beaten
fine dried breadcrumbs
Sauce:
150 ml (¼ pint) chicken
stock
3 heaped tablespoons
redcurrant jelly
grated rind and juice of 2
oranges
1 tablespoon lemon juice

Preparation time: 15 minutes
Cooking time: 50 minutes
Oven: 200°C, 400°F,
Gas Mark 6;
then 180°C, 350°F,
Gas Mark 4

1. Sprinkle the cutlets with salt and pepper. Dip in the egg, then coat in bread-crumbs. Arrange the cutlets side by side in a greased roasting tin.
2. Put all the sauce ingredients in a pan and heat, stirring, until smooth.
3. Pour half the sauce over and around the cutlets. Bake in a preheated oven for 30 minutes.
4. Add the remaining sauce, and reduce the oven temperature. Bake for a further 20 minutes or until the cutlets are a rich golden brown and the sauce is syrupy.

From the left: Onion soup gratinée; Fisherman's casserole; Cumberland cutlets

PAPRIKA BEEF

Serves 6

●

1 kg (2 lb) braising steak,
cut 2 cm (¾ inch) thick
2 teaspoons paprika
salt
freshly ground black
pepper
oil for frying
2 onions, peeled and thinly
sliced
100 g (4 oz) mushrooms,
sliced
1 large green pepper, cored,
seeded and sliced
300 ml (½ pint) beef stock
or thin gravy
1 tablespoon tomato purée

Preparation time: 20 minutes
Cooking time: about 2½ hours
Oven: 150°C, 300°F,
Gas Mark 2

---

1. Lay the meat on a board.
Mix together the paprika
and salt and pepper to taste
and sprinkle half over the
meat. Pound the seasoning
in, using the edge of a
saucer, then turn the meat
over and repeat the seasoning on the other side. Cut
the meat into 6 pieces.
2. Pour enough oil into a
frying pan to make a 3 mm
(⅛ inch) thick layer. Heat
until really hot, then add
the meat and brown on both
sides, turning once. Lift out
the meat.
3. Add the onions to the
pan and cook gently until
softened. Add the
mushrooms and green
pepper and cook for a
further 2 minutes.
4. Transfer the vegetable
mixture to a casserole and
place the meat on top.
5. Mix together the stock
or gravy and tomato purée

in the frying pan and bring
to the boil. Pour the
mixture into the casserole.
6. Cover and cook in a preheated oven for 2 hours.
Serve with boiled or
mashed potatoes.

TUNA LASAGNE

Serves 4-5

●

9 strips of lasagne pasta
50 g (2 oz) butter
½ onion, peeled and finely
chopped
½ green pepper, cored,
seeded and finely chopped
40 g (1½ oz) plain flour
600 ml (1 pint) milk
½ teaspoon mustard
powder
¼ teaspoon grated nutmeg
(optional)
salt
white pepper
2 teaspoons chopped fresh
parsley
3 tablespoons single cream
or top of milk
75 g (3 oz) mature cheese,
grated
1 × 200 g (7 oz) can tuna,
drained and flaked
2 hard-boiled eggs, shelled
and sliced

Preparation time: 20 minutes
Cooking time: 55-70 minutes
Oven: 190°C, 375°F,
Gas Mark 5

---

1. If using regular lasagne,
cook according to packet
directions.
2. Melt the butter in a
saucepan, add the onion
and cook, covered, for 5
minutes. Add the green
pepper and continue cook-
ing for 3-4 minutes.
3. Uncover and stir in the

flour, then gradually stir in
the milk. Add the mustard,
nutmeg and salt and pepper
to taste. Bring to the boil,
stirring, and simmer until

thickened.
4. Stir in the parsley,
cream, half of the cheese,
the tuna and eggs.
5. To assemble the lasagne,

put a thin layer of the tuna sauce on the bottom of a buttered 20 × 25 cm (8 × 10 inch) baking dish that is 5-7.5 cm (2-3 inches) deep.

Cover with 3 strips of pasta, then with another layer of sauce. Continue layering the ingredients, finishing up with the tuna sauce.

Sprinkle the remaining cheese over the Tuna lasagne.
6. Bake in a preheated oven for about 40 minutes or un-

From the left: Paprika beef; Tuna lasagne

til browned and bubbling. Cut into squares to serve.

From the left: Green and gold salad; Oven-fried chicken Maryland

GREEN AND GOLD SALAD

Serves 8-10

●

450 g (1 lb) frozen green beans
1 × 300 g (11½ oz) can sweetcorn with pimientos, drained
50 g (2 oz) stoned black or stuffed green olives, sliced
Dressing:
3 tablespoons corn or olive oil
2 tablespoons wine vinegar
2 teaspoons caster sugar
1 tablespoon chopped onion
salt
freshly ground black pepper

Preparation time: 10 minutes plus chilling
Cooking time: 5-8 minutes

1. Cook the beans in boiling salted water for 5-8 minutes or until barely tender. Drain and rinse under cold running water.
2. Tip the beans into a bowl and add the corn and olives.
3. Combine all the dressing ingredients in a screwtop jar and shake well.
4. Pour the dressing over the vegetables and stir well. Cover and chill before serving.

OVEN-FRIED CHICKEN MARYLAND

Serves 4

●

1.5 kg (3 lb) chicken, cut into quarters
50 g (2 oz) plain flour
½ teaspoon dried Herbes de Provence
salt
freshly ground black pepper
1 egg, beaten
dried breadcrumbs to coat
50 g (2 oz) butter or margarine
4 tablespoons oil

76

Lemon Pavlova Cake

Serves 8-10

●

4 large egg whites
¼ teaspoon cream of tartar,
or 1 teaspoon vinegar
pinch of salt (optional)
2 teaspoons cornflour
225 g (8 oz) caster sugar
1 teaspoon vanilla essence
Filling:
4 egg yolks
100 g (4 oz) caster sugar
grated rind of ½ lemon
3 tablespoons lemon juice
225 ml (8 fl oz) whipping
cream

---

*Preparation time: 15-20 minutes
plus cooling and chilling
Cooking time: 1-1¼ hours
Oven: 150°C, 300°F,
Gas Mark 2;
then 140°C, 275°F,
Gas Mark 1*

---

*Preparation time: 10 minutes
Cooking time: 35-45 minutes
Oven: 190°C, 375°F,
Gas Mark 5*

---

1. Coat the chicken in the flour seasoned with the herbs and salt and pepper. Dip into the egg, then coat with breadcrumbs.
2. Lay the pieces side by side in an oiled roasting tin and bake in a preheated oven for 5 minutes.
3. Melt the butter or margarine and oil in a pan and heat for 3 minutes.
4. Pour the butter mixture over the chicken and bake for a further 30-40 minutes or until golden brown. Baste once during cooking.

1. Put the egg whites and cream of tartar in a large mixing bowl. If using the vinegar instead of the cream of tartar, add the salt here. Start whisking at low speed until frothy, then increase the speed and whisk until stiff and glossy.
2. Mix the cornflour with the sugar. Add 1 tablespon at a time to the egg whites, beating until stiff after each addition. Beat in the vanilla essence, then beat in the vinegar, if used.
3. Spoon the meringue into two greased and bottom-lined 23 cm (9 inch) round loose-bottomed cake tins and smooth the tops. Alternatively, draw two 20 cm (8 inch) circles on greaseproof paper and lay each sheet of paper on a baking sheet; pipe or spoon the meringue onto the paper to make rounds.
4. Place in a preheated oven and reduce the heat. Bake for 45 minutes to 1 hour, changing the positon of the layers at half time, until the tops of the meringues feel really firm and crisp to the touch. Leave to cool completely.
5. To make the filling, put the egg yolks and sugar in a heavy pan and beat with a wooden spoon until creamy. Stir in the lemon rind and juice. Cook gently, stirring, until the mixture thickens to the consistency of lemon curd. Do not allow to boil.
6. Remove from the heat and allow to cool for 1-2 minutes, stirring, then turn into a bowl and leave to cool completely.
7. Whip the cream until thick and fold into the lemon mixture.
8. Put one meringue layer on a serving plate and spread over the filling. Top with the second meringue layer. Chill overnight.

Lemon pavlova cake

EVELYN ROSE AT HOME

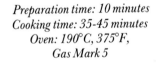

77

ZENA SKINNER

FISH AND CHEESE CRUMBLE

Serves 4

•

450 g (1 lb) cod fillet
150 ml (¼ pint) milk
1 egg yolk, beaten
1 tablespoon chopped fresh
parsley
salt
freshly ground black
pepper
2 large tomatoes, skinned
and sliced
Crumble:
40 g (1½ oz) butter or lard
100 g (4 oz) self-raising
flour
50 g (2 oz) Cheddar cheese,
grated
small pinch of cayenne
pepper

Preparation time: 15 minutes
Cooking time: 55 minutes
Oven: 180°C, 350°F,
Gas Mark 4

---

1. Put the fish into a frying pan, cutting it to fit if necessary, and pour over the milk. Cover and simmer gently for about 10 minutes or until the fish will flake easily when tested.
2. Remove the cod to a dish and flake, discarding any skin. Pour the milk into a small bowl and add the egg yolk, parsley and salt and pepper to taste. Stir well together.
3. Put the fish into a greased 900 ml (1½ pint) baking dish and pour over the milk mixture. Arrange the tomatoes evenly on the top.
4. To make the crumble, rub 25 g (1 oz) of the butter or lard into the flour until

has made well over 400 television appearances since the first in 1959. They include no fewer than nine long-running series on both BBC and ITV, such as *Town And Around, Ask Zena Skinner, Looking At Cooking, Know Your Onions* and *Bon Appetit*. On radio she has made guest appearances on *Woman's Hour, You And Yours* and *Tuesday Call*, was a castaway on *Desert Island Discs*, and she has written eight cookbooks for BBC Publications. Her travels include lecture tours of Africa and the West Indies.

---

the mixture resembles breadcrumbs. Stir in the cheese, cayenne pepper and salt to taste.
5. Sprinkle the crumble over the tomatoes, spreading it out evenly. Flake the remaining butter or lard over the crumble.
6. Bake in a preheated oven for about 35 minutes, then increase the temperature slightly to brown the top for a further 10 minutes.

BEEF BROTH

Serves 4-6

•

500 g (1¼ lb) shin of beef,
skin and gristle removed,
cut into small pieces
2 beef stock cubes dissolved
in 300 ml (½ pint) boiling
water
1.2 litres (2 pints) cold
water
2 carrots, peeled and diced
1 small turnip, peeled and
diced
1 onion, peeled and diced
1 leek, diced
25 g (1 oz) pearl barley
salt
freshly ground black
pepper
chopped fresh parsley, to
garnish

Preparation time: 15 minutes
Cooking time: 2¼ hours

1. Put the meat, stock cubes and cold water in a pan and bring slowly to the boil. Skim off any scum, then simmer gently for 1 hour.
2. Add the vegetables and barley and simmer for a further 1 hour.
3. Add seasoning to taste. Serve sprinkled with parsley.

POTATO SALAD

Serves 4

•

175 ml (6 fl oz) mayonnaise
85 ml (3 fl oz) plain
unsweetened yogurt
½ teaspoon curry powder
1 teaspoon grated onion
2 tablespoons chopped
fresh parsley
salt
freshly ground black
pepper
450 g (1 lb) potatoes,
peeled, cooked and sliced

Preparation time: 10 minutes
plus cooking potatoes

---

1. Mix together the mayonnaise, yogurt, curry powder, onion, parsley and salt and pepper to taste.
2. Fold in the cold potatoes.

Clockwise from top right: Potato salad; Beef broth; Fish and cheese crumble

MOTHER'S JUGGED HARE

Serves 4-6

●

1 small hare, jointed
50-100 g (2-4 oz) plain flour
salt
freshly ground black
pepper
50 g (2 oz) dripping
4 cloves
1 onion, peeled and halved
1 bouquet garni
600 ml (1 pint) stock
1-2 wineglasses port
redcurrant jelly, to serve

Preparation time: 10 minutes
Cooking time: 2¼-2¾ hours
Oven: 150°C, 300°F,
Gas Mark 2

---

1. Coat the hare joints with the flour seasoned with salt and pepper.

2. Heat the dripping in a frying pan, brown the joints on all sides and transfer to a deep casserole.

3. Stick the cloves into the onion halves and add to the casserole with the bouquet garni.

4. Put any remaining flour into the frying pan and cook until it browns, then gradually stir in the stock. Simmer, stirring, until thickened.

5. Pour the stock mixture over the hare, adding a little extra stock if necessary to cover the joints. Cover and cook in a preheated oven for about 2-2½ hours or until the hare is tender.

6. About 30 minutes before the hare is ready, discard the onion and bouquet garni and stir in the port.

7. Serve hot, with redcurrant jelly.

ZENA'S STEAK AND KIDNEY PIE

Serves 4

●

750 g (1½ lb) skirt or chuck
and blade beef, cut into
small cubes
100 g (4 oz) ox kidney,
cored and cut into small
cubes
25 g (1 oz) plain flour
salt
freshly ground black
pepper
225 g (8 oz) rough puff
pastry

*Preparation time: 20 minutes
plus making pastry
Cooking time: about 2 hours
Oven: 220°C, 425°F,
Gas Mark 7*

1. Toss the beef and kidney in the flour seasoned with salt and pepper. Put into a saucepan and add enough water just to cover the meat.
2. Cook gently until the meat is tender.
3. Turn into a 900 ml (1½ pint) pie dish, placing a funnel in the centre if liked.
4. Roll out the pastry and use to cover the pie.
5. Place on a baking sheet and bake in a preheated oven for about 45 minutes or until the pastry is a rich golden brown. Serve hot.

From the left: Mother's jugged hare; Zena's steak and kidney pie

ZENA SKINNER ▦ AT HOME

GOOSEBERRY AND STRAWBERRY JAM

Makes about 1.75 kg (4 lb)

•

1 kg (2 lb) gooseberries, topped and tailed
2 kg (4 lb) strawberries, hulled
3 kg (6 lb) sugar

Preparation time: 10 minutes
Cooking time: 30-45 minutes

---

1. Cut the gooseberries in half with scissors. Put them in a preserving pan or large saucepan and add enough water just to cover the fruit. Simmer until soft.
2. Add the strawberries and sugar and stir to dissolve the sugar. Bring to the boil and boil until setting point is reached.
3. Allow the jam to cool slightly, then skim off any scum and pot into hot jars. Seal and label.

RHUBARB CHEESECAKE

Serves 4-6

•

50 g (2 oz) butter
25 g (1 oz) demerara sugar
225 g (8 oz) digestive biscuits, crushed
Filling:
225 g (8 oz) early rhubarb, cut into 1 cm (½ inch) thick slices
75 g (3 oz) caster sugar
2 eggs, beaten
100 g (4 oz) cottage cheese, sieved
65 ml (2½ fl oz) whipping cream

Preparation time: 15 minutes plus chilling
Cooking time: 15 minutes

---

1. Melt the butter in a saucepan and stir in the sugar and biscuits. Mix well together, then press into a greased 18 cm (7 inch) pie plate. Chill while making the filling.
2. Put the rhubarb and sugar in a saucepan and stew very gently until soft. Remove from the heat and mash well with a fork. Add the eggs and stir until the mixture thickens. Allow to cool.
3. Stir the cottage cheese into the rhubarb mixture. Whip the cream until thick and fold it in.
4. Pour the filling into the pie plate. Chill well before serving.

MALT FRUIT LOAF

Makes a 450 g (1 lb) loaf
●
225 g (8 oz) self-raising
flour
1 heaped teaspoon caster
sugar
100 g (4 oz) raisins or
sultanas
1 tablespoon malt extract
1 rounded tablespoon
golden syrup
120 ml (4 fl oz) milk

Preparation time: 10 minutes
Cooking time: 50-60 minutes
Oven: 170°C, 325°F,
Gas Mark 3

1. Sift the flour into a bowl and stir in the sugar and raisins or sultanas.
2. Melt the malt extract and golden syrup in a saucepan, then add to the flour mixture with about three-quarters of the milk. Stir well together, adding the remaining milk if necessary to make a fairly soft dough.
3. Turn into a greased and lined 450 g (1 lb) loaf tin. Bake in a preheated oven for about 50 minutes to 1 hour.
4. Cool on a wire rack.

From the left: Gooseberry and strawberry jam; Rhubarb cheesecake; Malt fruit loaf

83

GRACE MULLIGAN

HOT BEETROOT SOUP

Serves 6
•
50 g (2 oz) butter or margarine
450 g (1 lb) raw beetroot, diced
450 g (1 lb) potatoes, diced
2 onions, chopped
1.5-1.75 litres (2½-3 pints) strong chicken stock
salt
freshly ground black pepper
To garnish:
plain unsweetened yogurt or soured cream

who took over as presenter of Yorkshire TV's *Farmhouse Kitchen* in 1982, is a Scot who studied home economy in Edinburgh and was a secondary school teacher before marrying her GP husband. When they came south of the border 20 years ago she joined the local Women's Institute and it was through her work as judge and demonstrator that she first made a TV guest appearance in 1980. She travels all over the country lecturing and writes a syndicated newspaper cookery column.

Preparation time: 15 minutes
Cooking time: 35 minutes

1 Melt the butter in a large saucepan and cook the vegetables gently for about 5 minutes with the lid on.
2. Stir in the stock, bring to the boil and simmer until the beetroot is cooked.
3. Cool the soup and purée in a liquidizer. Return to the pan. Taste and adjust the seasoning.
4. Before serving, bring the soup to boiling point. Serve with a swirl of yogurt or soured cream in each bowl.

COLEY WITH A HOT CUCUMBER SAUCE

Serves 4
•
4 small fillets of fresh coley, skinned
about 300 ml (½ pint) milk
Sauce:
1 small cucumber
salt
1 × 150 ml (¼ pint) carton of single cream
150 ml (¼ pint) plain unsweetened yogurt
1 teaspoon caster sugar
freshly ground white pepper
To garnish:
chopped parsley
slices of lemon

Preparation time: 15 minutes, plus standing
Cooking time: 20-25 minutes

1. Put the coley in a shallow pan, barely cover with milk and poach gently for 15 to 20 minutes.
2. Drain off the milk and keep the fish hot.
3. Grate the entire cucumber coarsely. Spread out in a flat shallow dish. Sprinkle with salt and leave for 20 minutes. Strain.
4. Turn the pulp into a small saucepan. Stir in the cream and yogurt. Add the sugar and pepper.
5. When the mixture starts to bubble, turn it into a jug to serve separately.
6. Garnish the fish with parsley and lemon slices.

Left: Hot beetroot soup; right: Coley with a hot cucumber sauce

HAM, EGG AND ONION FLAN

Serves 4

•

150 g (5 oz) frozen wholewheat or white shortcrust pastry, thawed
Filling:
25 g (1 oz) ham fat or lard
1 small onion, finely chopped
100 g (4 oz) cooked ham
2 eggs, beaten
300 ml (½ pint) milk
salt
freshly ground black pepper
50 g (2 oz) Cheddar cheese, grated

Preparation time: 15 minutes
Cooking time: 35 minutes
Oven: 200°C, 400°F, Gas Mark 6;
then 180°C, 350°F, Gas Mark 4

---

1. Using a floured board, roll out the pastry to fit a 20 cm (8 inch) flan tin, or a ring set on a baking sheet or a flan dish.
2. Heat the fat and fry the onion gently to soften it.
3. Put the onion and ham in the flan.
4. Mix the eggs, milk and seasoning and strain into the flan.
5. Sprinkle the cheese on top.
6. Bake near the top of the oven for 20 minutes. Then reduce the oven temperature for another 10 minutes until cooked.

SWEET PICKLED PRUNES

•

225 g (8 oz) dried prunes
225 g (8 oz) soft brown sugar
300 ml (½ pint) malt vinegar
150 ml (¼ pint) water
5 cm (2 inch) piece of cinnamon

Preparation time: 10 minutes plus standing overnight
Cooking time: about 10 minutes

These can be eaten immediately, but will keep for a year. They are good with cold meat and a good alternative to black olives on pizza.
1. Put the prunes in a bowl, add the sugar, vinegar, water and cinnamon piece.

Cover and leave overnight.
2. Next day, turn everything into a saucepan. Simmer until the prunes are tender, about 10 minutes. Leave to cool.
3. Remove the prunes, split and remove the stones.
4. Pack the prunes into jars.
5. Return the pan of syrup to the heat. Simmer for 1 minute and pour over the prunes to cover.
6. Put on vinegar-proof lids, label and store.

OXTAIL MOULD

Serves 4
●
1 oxtail
225 g (8 oz) bacon in a piece
or bacon pieces
1 small onion
4 cloves
salt
freshly ground black
pepper

Preparation time: 20 minutes
Cooking time: 3 hours, or 1 hour
in a pressure cooker

1. Wash and joint the oxtail.
2. Put in a pan, with the bacon cut in chunks and the onion stuck with the cloves. Cover with water. Cover and simmer gently for 3 hours. Or pressure cook for 1 hour.

3. Strain off the liquid and remove the onion.
4. Take all meat from the bones and cut it up, discarding fat. Chop the bacon.
5. Return the strained liquid and meat to the pan. Season with salt and pepper. Bring to the boil.
6. Pour into a mould and leave to set.
7. Serve the Oxtail mould cold with hot creamed potatoes.

From the left: Ham, egg and onion flan; Sweet pickled prunes; Oxtail mould

From the left: Yorkshire curd tart; Short time bread; Savoury drop scones or pancakes

YORKSHIRE CURD TART

Serves 4

●

1.2 litres (2 pints) milk
(Channel Islands milk is
best)
1 teaspoon Epsom salts
175 g (6 oz) frozen
shortcrust pastry, thawed
25 g (1 oz) butter or
margarine
25 g (1 oz) currants, washed
1 egg (size 1), beaten
1 tablespoon caster sugar
1 tablespoon golden syrup
1 tablespoon rum

Preparation time: 20 minutes
Cooking time: about 35 minutes
Oven: 200°C, 400°F,
Gas Mark 6

---

1. To make the curd, bring the milk to boiling point. Remove from the heat and add the Epsom salts.
2. Leave for a few minutes for curds to form. Stir well and strain. This makes enough curd for two 15-18 cm (6-7 inch) flans. It will keep in the refrigerator for 1 week.
3. Roll out the pastry to line an 18 cm (7 inch) flan ring placed on a greased baking sheet.
4. Combine the remaining ingredients and fill the pastry case.
5. Bake above the middle of the oven for 30 minutes, until the pastry is cooked and the filling firm and golden.

SHORT TIME BREAD

Makes 1 loaf or 6 buns

●

15 g (½ oz) fresh yeast or 7 g
(¼ oz) dried yeast
1 × 25 mg vitamin C tablet,
crushed (obtainable from
chemists, also called
ascorbic acid)
½ teaspoon sugar
approximately 150 ml (¼
pint) warm water
225 g (8 oz) strong plain
flour
½ teaspoon salt
15 g (½ oz) margarine

Preparation time: 20 minutes,
plus proving
Cooking time: 10-30 minutes
Oven: 220°C, 425°F,
Gas Mark 7

---

1. Blend together the yeast, crushed vitamin C tablet and half of the water. If using dried yeast, add sugar and wait until it froths up before using.
2. Sift the flour and salt and rub in the margarine.
3. Pour the yeast liquid into the dry ingredients and mix well.
4. Add sufficient warm water to make a soft, beatable dough.
5. Beat the dough until it leaves the sides of the bowl clean.
6. Turn out on to a lightly-floured board and knead for 10 minutes until smooth.
7. Allow the dough to rest for 5 minutes, covered lightly.
8. Shape into bread buns or cottage loaf, twist or plait and put on a greased baking sheet. Cover with a damp cloth or greased polythene, and leave in a warm place to rise until doubled in size.
9. Bake near the top of the oven. Bread buns take 10 to 12 minutes. Loaves take 25 to 30 minutes.

Variation:
Use 225 g (8 oz) whole-wheat flour, or half whole-wheat and half white flour instead of all white.

SAVOURY DROP SCONES OR PANCAKES

Makes about 15

●

225 g (8 oz) plain white or
wholewheat flour
1 teaspoon cream of tartar
½ teaspoon bicarbonate of
soda
pinch of salt
2 teaspoons onion, finely
chopped
1 egg
approximately 150 ml (¼
pint) milk
knob of beef suet, lard or
margarine for greasing

Preparation time: 10 minutes
Cooking time: approximately 10
minutes

---

1. Put the flour in a bowl. Sift the cream of tartar, bicarbonate of soda and salt. Mix in the onion.
2. Mix to a thick pouring batter with the egg and milk.
3. Heat the girdle or heavy frying pan and grease it.
4. Drop spoonfuls of batter on the girdle. When bubbles appear, turn over and cook the other side.
5. Cool the scones in a towel. This stops them drying out.

DOROTHY SLEIGHTHOLME

LAMB AND LENTIL HOTPOT

Serves 4

•

100 g (4 oz) lentils
750 g (1½ lb) middle neck of lamb
1 tablespoon plain flour
40 g (1½ oz) lard
2 medium onions, chopped
450 g (1 lb) carrots, thinly sliced
2 beef stock cubes
salt
freshly ground black pepper
sprig of fresh rosemary or 1 teaspoon dried rosemary or thyme, well crushed
chopped parsley

a Yorkshire farmer's daughter, made her first television appearance as the result of winning a cookery contest. Guest appearances on Yorkshire television's *Farmhouse Kitchen* made her so popular with viewers that she soon took over the series and in 13 years she presented over 150 programmes. She learned her cooking skills helping to prepare family meals. Long before her TV career began she was winning prizes at local shows, demonstrating at Women's Institutes and teaching at evening classes.

Preparation time: 15 minutes, plus soaking
Cooking time: 1½-1¾ hours
Oven: 180°C, 350°F, Gas Mark 4

1. Place the lentils in a basin and cover with boiling water. Leave for one hour, then drain, reserving the water.

2. Trim excess fat from the meat.
3. Put flour on a plate or in a clean bag and thoroughly coat the meat.
4. Melt half the lard in a large frying pan. Fry the onions and carrots for 3 minutes. Lift them out into a casserole, saving the fat.
5. Add the remaining lard to the pan and fry the meat until brown on both sides.

Add to the casserole.
6. Crumble the beef stock cubes into the casserole.
7. Make the lentil water up to 600 ml (1 pint) with fresh cold water and pour this over the meat. Add salt and pepper to taste and rosemary or thyme.
8. Cover the casserole and cook in the centre of the oven for 1¼ to 1½ hours until the meat is tender.
9. Sprinkle with chopped parsley.
10. Serve with a lightly-cooked green vegetable.

Below: Lamb and lentil hotpot; right; Creamy onion pie with cheese pastry

CREAMY ONION PIE

Serves 4

●

1 quantity cheese pastry,
uncooked (see below)
225 ml (8 fl oz) milk
1 small bay leaf
6 to 8 peppercorns
40 g (1½ oz) butter
2 large onions, thinly sliced
65 g (2½ oz) fresh white or
wholewheat breadcrumbs
2 eggs, beaten
salt
freshly ground black
pepper
1 teaspoon Worcestershire
sauce
2 tablespoons double cream
a little grated cheese
(optional)

Preparation time: 20 minutes
Cooking time: 35 minutes
Oven: 200°C, 400°F,
Gas Mark 6

---

1. Use the pastry to line a
20 cm (8 inch) flan ring on a
baking sheet.
2. Place the milk, bay leaf
and peppercorns in a pan,
and heat to nearly boiling.
Remove from the heat and
infuse for 5 minutes.
3. Melt the butter and cook
the onions until soft.
4. Place the breadcrumbs
in a large bowl, strain the
milk and pour it over.
5. Add the onions and
butter, eggs, seasoning and
sauce. Stir in the cream.
6. Pour into the pastry case

and bake for about 25
minutes until the pastry is
golden and the filling is set.
7. Sprinkle grated cheese
on top and place under
medium grill to finish.

CHEESEPASTRY

●

225 g (8 oz) plain white or
wholewheat flour
½ level teaspoon salt
½ level teaspoon dry
mustard
pinch of cayenne pepper
75 g (3 oz) hard margarine
or vegetable fat
75 g (3 oz) well-flavoured
cheese, finely grated
1 egg yolk
2 tablespoons water (3 for
wholewheat pastry)

1. Sift or mix flour, salt,
mustard and cayenne
pepper.
2. Rub in the margarine
with fingertips until the
mixture is like bread-
crumbs. Mix in the cheese.
3. Mix the egg yolk with
the water and stir it into the
flour mixture with a round-
ended knife.
4. Knead lightly until
smooth and a firm dough is
formed.

91

CHICKEN WITH APPLE

Serves 4-6

•

1 chicken, jointed
2 tablespoons plain flour
salt
freshly ground black
pepper
50 g (2 oz) bacon fat
1 large onion, peeled and
sliced
1 large carrot, peeled and
sliced
2 sharp eating apples,
peeled, cored and
quartered
225 g (8 oz) shelled fresh or
frozen peas
300 ml (½ pint) cider
150 ml (¼ pint) chicken
giblet stock
chopped fresh parsley, to
garnish

Preparation time: 15 minutes
Cooking time: 50-55 minutes

---

1. Toss the chicken joints in the flour seasoned with salt and pepper. Heat the fat in a frying pan and brown the chicken joints on all sides. Remove from the pan and set aside.
2. Coat the onion and carrot in the remaining flour and add to the pan. Cook the vegetables, stirring, for 1 minute.
3. Return the chicken joints to the pan, and add the apple quarters and fresh peas. Pour over the cider and stock. Bring to the boil, then cover and simmer for 30 minutes.
4. If using frozen peas, add them and cook for a further 10 minutes.
5. Serve sprinkled with chopped parsley.

RABBIT WITH MUSTARD

Serves 4-5

•

1 rabbit, jointed
100 g (4 oz) bacon, in 1
piece or 2 thick slices
25 g (1 oz) bacon fat or
dripping
6 small onions, peeled
3½ tablespoons wholemeal
or plain flour
600 ml (1 pint) chicken
stock
2 teaspoons French
mustard
salt
freshly ground black
pepper
15 g (½ oz) soft butter, to
thicken sauce
3 tablespoons cream or
natural yogurt
1 tablespoon chopped
parsley

Preparation time: 15 minutes,
plus soaking
Cooking time: 1¼ hours

---

1. Soak the rabbit in salted water for 2 or 3 hours, then drain and pat dry.
2. Remove rind and cut the bacon into small pieces.
3. Heat the fat in a large saucepan and fry the bacon and onions for 2 or 3 minutes. Transfer them from the pan to a plate.
4. Brown the rabbit joints in the fat and lift out on to the plate.
5. Stir 2 tablespoons of the flour into the fat and juices now in the pan and cook, stirring, for 1 to 2 minutes.
6. Remove the pan from the heat and gradually blend in the stock and mustard. Return the pan to the heat and boil, stirring constantly.

Keep stirring while it simmers for 1 to 2 minutes.
7. Return the rabbit, bacon and onions to the pan. Add salt and pepper to taste.

8. Cover the pan and simmer for 1 hour.
9. Remove the rabbit joints and arrange them on the warmed dish.

10. If the sauce needs thickening, strain it into a small pan, spreading the contents of the strainer over the rabbit. Blend together the flour and the remaining butter and whisk small bits into the sauce. Bring to the boil and cook gently for 2 minutes.

11. Stir cream or yogurt, and chopped parsley into the sauce and pour over the rabbit joints. Serve the dish at once.

From the left: Chicken with apple; Rabbit with mustard

93

OLDFASHIONED SPICE BREAD

Makes 10-12 slices

•

2 teaspoons dried yeast, or
15 g (½ oz) fresh yeast
½ teaspoon sugar
150 ml (¼ pint) tepid milk
350 g (12 oz) plain flour
½ teaspoon salt
½ teaspoon mixed spice
½ teaspoon cinnamon
½ teaspoon bicarbonate of
soda
50 g (2 oz) margarine
50 g (2 oz) lard
175 g (6 oz) soft brown
sugar
100 g (4 oz) currants
100 g (4 oz) sultanas
50 g (2 oz) chopped candied
peel
1 egg, beaten
2 teaspoons dark treacle

Preparation time: 20 minutes
Cooking time: 1 ½ hours
Oven: 150°C, 300°F,
Gas Mark 2

---

1. Grease and base-line a
900 g (2 lb) loaf tin.
2. Add the dried yeast and
sugar to the milk, stir and
leave until frothy (note
manufacturer's directions).
If using fresh yeast, stir into
the milk with the sugar and
use at once.
3. Sift together the flour,
salt, spices and bicarbonate
of soda.
4. Rub the fats into the
flour, add the soft brown
sugar and dried fruit.
5. Add the yeast mixture,
egg and treacle. Mix to-
gether adding a little more
milk, if necessary, to make a
dropping consistency.
6. Spoon into the loaf tin
and level the top.

7. Bake for 1½ hours, until
firm on top and leaving the
sides of the tin.
8. Leave in the tin for about
10 minutes, then remove
and cool on a wire tray.
9. The bread is particularly
good with Wensleydale
cheese.

KEDGEREE

Serves 4

•

100 g (4 oz) long grain rice
350 g (12 oz) smoked
haddock fillet
300 ml (½ pint) milk and
water mixed
50 g (2 oz) butter
2 tablespoons cream or top
of milk
2 hard-boiled eggs, 1
chopped and 1 sliced
freshly ground black
pepper
chopped fresh parsley

Preparation time: 10 minutes
Cooking time: 25-30 minutes

---

1. Cook the rice in boiling
salted water until just
tender.
2. Poach the haddock in
the milk and water until just
beginning to flake. Drain,
then flake roughly,
discarding the skin.
3. Drain the rice in a sieve,
and pour over boiling water
to rinse off excess starch.
4. Return the rice to the
pan and add the fish, butter,
cream, chopped egg, and
pepper to taste. Heat
through gently. If too firm,
add a little more cream.
5. Serve in a warmed dish
garnished with the sliced
egg and parsley.

From the left: Old-fashioned
spice bread; Kedgeree

DOROTHY SLEIGHTHOLME AT HOME

BAKED ALASKA

Serves 4

•

2 eggs
65 g (2½ oz) vanilla or caster sugar
65 g (2½ oz) plain flour
2 tablespoons sherry or fruit juice
1 family-size block of ice cream, about 485 g (17 oz) size
Meringue:
3 egg whites
120 g (4½ oz) caster sugar

Preparation time: 30 minutes, plus cooling
Cooking time: 25 minutes
Oven: 180°C, 350°F, Gas Mark 4;
then 220°C, 425°F, Gas Mark 7

---

1. Put the eggs and sugar into a bowl and whisk over a pan of hot water until the mixture is pale and thick. Remove the bowl from the heat and continue whisking until the beaters will leave a trail in the mixture.
2. Sift the flour on top of the mixture and fold it in. Pour into a greased and lined 18 × 28 cm (7 × 11 inch) Swiss roll tin and spread to fill it evenly.
3. Bake in a preheated oven for about 20 minutes or until firm to the touch and shrinking slightly from the sides of the tin.
4. Cool on a wire tray, then peel off the lining paper.
5. Trim the sponge so that when the ice cream is placed on it there is at least 1 cm (½ inch) of cake all around the edge. Save the rest of the cake for tea.
6. Place the sponge on a heatproof dish and sprinkle over the sherry or fruit juice. Place the ice cream on top.
7. To make the meringue, whisk the egg whites until stiff and fold in the sugar. Spread the meringue over the ice cream to cover it completely, sealing it to the cake on all sides.
8. Increase the oven temperature and bake for about 4 minutes, or until the meringue is tinged gold. Serve immediately.

BREAD AND BUTTER PUDDING

Serves 3-4

•

150 g (5 oz) stale bread (without crusts)
butter
50 g (2 oz) sultanas
1 teaspoon candied peel
2 tablespoons demerara or plain white sugar
1 egg (size 1)
300 ml (½ pint) milk
nutmeg, grated

Preparation time: 15 minutes, plus soaking
Cooking time: 1 hour
Oven: 180°C, 350°F, Gas Mark 4

This is delicious made from stale Hot Cross Buns, Bun Loaf, or Sally Lunn. Where fruit is already incorporated in the loaf or buns, extra sultanas and candied peel are not needed, nor is it necessary to remove crusts.
1. Butter a 1 litre (1½ pint) pie dish.
2. Slice the bread, butter it and cut into small pieces.

3. Place half the bread in the pie dish, sprinkle on the fruit and half the sugar. Cover with the remaining bread.
4. Beat the egg and milk, pour over the bread and leave to soak for 30 minutes.
5. Sprinkle the remaining

96

sugar and a little grated nutmeg on top.

6. Bake the Bread and butter pudding for about 1 hour until it is just set.

From the left: Baked Alaska; Bread and butter pudding

97

SHIRLEY GOODE

CHICKEN AND BARLEY SOUP

Serves 4

•

450 g (1 lb) chicken pieces such as wings, neck and giblets
600 ml (1 pint) chicken stock
2 carrots, peeled and diced
1 potato, peeled and diced
1 celery stalk with leaves, chopped
2 onions, peeled and chopped
freshly ground black pepper
75-100 g (3-4 oz) pearl barley, cooked or uncooked
few mushroom stalks
plenty of chopped fresh herbs, e.g. parsley, tarragon, oregano

---

Preparation time: 15 minutes
Cooking time: 1¾ hours

This is a dish that uses up all the 'unusable' parts of a chicken: wings, neck, giblets can all go in this soup.
1. Put the chicken pieces in a large pan with the stock. Bring to the boil, skimming off the scum from the surface, then add the vegetables and pepper to taste. Partly cover the pan and simmer the chicken gently for 30 minutes.
2. Add the barley and mushroom stalks and continue simmering for 1 hour (if using cooked barley, simmer for only 30 minutes).
3. Remove the chicken pieces with a slotted spoon. Discard all skin, bone and gristle, and return any meat to the soup. Finely chop the liver and add to the soup.

earned her reputation for making a little money go a long way in the kitchen with her 'pound-stretcher fare' item on *Pebble Mill At One* and in 1986 she began her own series *The Goode Kitchen* on BBC1. Her ideas on economical cooking came from bringing up four children on a tight budget and her articles in local papers led to lectures and television appearances. She has written for *Good Housekeeping, Family Circle* and *Home and Freezer Digest* and contributes a weekly column to the *Yorkshire Evening Post*.

Stir in the finely chopped fresh herbs.
4. Reheat briefly and serve hot.

FISH AND RED BEAN SALAD

Serves 4

•

450 g (1 lb) white fish (coley, cod, haddock)
225 g (8 oz) red kidney beans, cooked
225 g (8 oz) sweetcorn, cooked
1 large green pepper, seeded and diced

Preparation time: 10 minutes, plus cooling
Cooking time: 10 minutes

Here's a colourful dish which I've re-named 'Grandma's Jewels' as it's a proper little treasure trove of good things to eat.
1. Place the fish in a pan, cover with water and simmer until cooked.
2. Remove the bones and skin and fork into flakes. Toss with all the other ingredients.
3. Serve cold with a lemony dressing (oil, preferably olive oil, and lemon juice, in proportion of 3:1, and

freshly ground black pepper), crisp green salad and hot crusty bread with garlic butter.

CRUNCHY CAULIFLOWER SALAD

Serves 4

•

1 small cauliflower
1 carrot, finely sliced
1 onion, finely chopped
4 tomatoes, skinned and sliced
French dressing

Preparation time: 5 minutes

---

1. Wash the cauliflower and break it into small florets. In a large bowl, mix all the ingredients together and toss in the dressing.

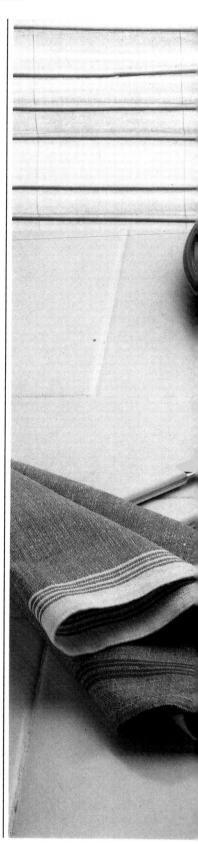

Clockwise from top left: Chicken and barley soup; Crunchy cauliflower salad; Fish and red bean salad

THE GOODE CASSOULET

Serves 4-6

●

225 g (8 oz) dried haricot or
butter beans, soaked
overnight
600 ml (1 pint) chicken
stock
1 pork shank
chicken pieces (winglets,
etc.)
2-4 cooked garlic sausages
(the long thin variety),
sliced
1 carrot, thinly sliced
1 onion, thinly sliced
1 dessertspoon clear honey
50 g (2 oz) tomato purée
2 tablespoons chopped
mixed fresh herbs, or 1
teaspoon dried mixed herbs
1 bay leaf
2 slices of bread, crumbled
freshly ground black
pepper

*Preparation time: 25 minutes
plus soaking
Cooking time: 3 1/2 hours
Oven: 150°C, 300°F,
Gas Mark 2*

1. Drain the beans and put
them in a saucepan. Add
the stock, bring to the boil
and simmer for 1 hour.
Drain, reserving the liquid.
2. Layer the beans, pork,
chicken, sausages, carrot
and onion in a casserole.
Mix together the honey,
tomato purée and reserved
bean liquid and pour over.
3. Cover and cook in a preheated oven for 1 1/2 hours.
4. Remove the lid.
Combine the herbs, bread
crumbs and pepper and
sprinkle over the cassoulet.
Cook for a further 1 hour.
5. Serve from the casserole.

LAMB AND LENTIL CASSEROLE

Serves 4

●

100 g (4 oz) green lentils
300 ml (½ pint) boiling beef
stock
1 onion, peeled and
chopped
2 carrots, peeled and sliced
4 small potatoes, sliced
350 g (12 oz) lean boneless
lamb, cubed
salt
freshly ground black
pepper
1 tablespoon redcurrant
jelly
chopped fresh parsley, to
garnish

---

*Preparation time: 20 minutes
Cooking time: 1½ hours
Oven: 180°C, 350°F,
Gas Mark 4*

---

1. Put the lentils in a casserole and pour over the stock. Add the vegetables, lamb, and salt and pepper to taste.
2. Cover and cook in a preheated oven for about 1½ hours or until the meat and vegetables are tender.
3. About 15 minutes before the end of the cooking time, stir in the redcurrant jelly. Add a little water if the casserole seems dry.
4. Serve sprinkled with parsley.

---

*Left: The Goode cassoulet; right;
Lamb and lentil casserole*

SHIRLEY GOODE ▌▌▌ AT HOME

101

CURD CHEESE

Makes 175-225 g (6-8 oz)

●

600 ml (1 pint) milk
2 tablespoons dried milk
powder
1 dessertspoon rennet
essence

---

*Preparation time: 10 minutes
plus setting and draining*

---

1. Heat the milk to blood heat, then stir in the milk powder. Remove from the heat and add the rennet essence. Stir thoroughly, then leave to stand until set.
2. Cut the set mixture into squares with a knife and tip it into a muslin-lined sieve placed over a bowl. Tie up the corners of the muslin and suspend the bag over the bowl. Leave overnight to drain off the whey.
3. The next day, transfer the cheese to a bowl and cover. Store in the refrigerator for up to 1 week.
4. The whey can be used instead of water in breadmaking, or you can make it up into milk again with dried milk powder.

From the left: Curd cheese; Marrow and ginger sorbet; Carrot cake

MARROW AND GINGER SORBET

Serves 4

●

450 g (1 lb) marrow, peeled, seeded and chopped
15 g (½ oz) preserved ginger, chopped
50 g (2 oz) sugar
2 teaspoons powdered gelatine
2 egg whites

---

*Preparation time: 15 minutes
plus freezing
Cooking time: 15-20 minutes*

---

1. Poach the marrow in a little water until soft. Drain well, then put into a blender or food processor with the ginger and blend to a smooth purée.
2. Measure 450 ml (¾ pint) of the marrow and ginger purée into a pan and add the sugar and gelatine. Heat gently, stirring to dissolve the sugar and gelatine.
3. Pour into a metal dish and allow to cool, then freeze until firm around the edges.
4. Beat the frozen sides into the middle with a fork to a frozen mush. Whisk the egg whites until stiff and fold into the mush. Cover and freeze until firm.
5. About 15 minutes before serving, remove the sorbet to the refrigerator and allow it to soften. Serve with a slice of melon as a starter.

CARROT CAKE

Makes a 20 cm (8 inch) ring cake

●

100 g (4 oz) sugar
100 g (4 oz) soft margarine
2 eggs
1 tablespoon black treacle
½ teaspoon baking powder
175 g (6 oz) self-raising flour
1 teaspoon ground cinnamon
175 g (6 oz) carrots, peeled and finely grated
50 g (2 oz) walnuts, chopped
Icing:
175 g (6 oz) low-fat curd cheese
50 g (2 oz) butter
175 g (6 oz) icing sugar

---

*Preparation time: 20 minutes
Cooking time: 1 hour
Oven: 180°C, 350°F,
Gas Mark 4*

---

1. Grease and flour a 20 cm (8 inch) ring mould. Set aside.
2. Beat the sugar and margarine together until light and fluffy. Beat in the eggs and treacle. Sift together the baking powder, flour and cinnamon and fold into the mixture.
3. Add the carrots and walnuts and mix in thoroughly.
4. Put the mixture into the ring mould and level the surface. Bake in a preheated oven for 1 hour.
5. To make the icing, beat together the cheese and butter until smooth. Sift in the icing sugar and beat in well.
6. Cool the cake on a wire rack. When cold, cover the top with the icing.

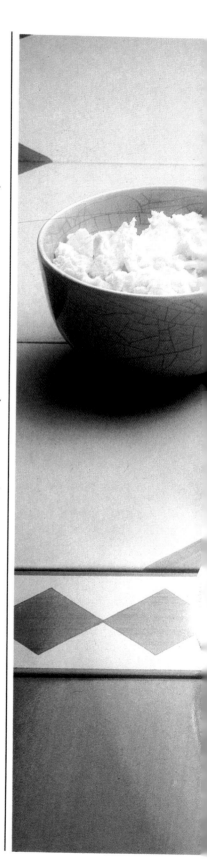

102

MICHAEL BARRY

LAMB AND FRUIT KEBABS

Makes 1 kebab per person

•

For each kebab:
175 g (6 oz) lamb, cubed
juice and rind of 1 lemon
pinch of cinnamon or
allspice
¼ green pepper, deseeded
and cut into 2½ cm (1 inch)
squares
4 pineapple cubes (fresh or
tinned)
4 apricot halves or peach
quarters (fresh or tinned)
juice and rind of 1 orange
salt
freshly ground black
pepper

---

*Preparation time: 25 minutes,
plus marinating
Cooking time: 8 minutes*

Exotic and delicious, these
kebabs are best served with
rice – saffron pilau make
them really special.
1. Marinate the lamb in the
lemon juice and cinnamon
for 2 hours.
2. Using either metal or
wood skewers, prepare each
kebab by threading on in
turn a chunk of pepper,
then lamb, then pineapple,
then apricot, and so on,
finishing with a piece of
pepper.
3. Grill the kebabs for 3
minutes, then turn and grill
for 4-5 minutes longer.
Meanwhile, bring the
grated rind of lemon and
orange to the boil in the
orange juice and simmer for
2 minutes.
4. Add the marinade and
all the other juices and
season well. Serve separately with the kebabs.

earned his reputation as the 'Crafty Cook' by
broadcasting on London's Capital Radio, putting
across the message that food can be fun. He brought
his fresh, no-nonsense approach in cooking to
television as a regular contributor to *TV-AM*,
demonstrating simple and delicious recipes, before
becoming presenter of the BBC magazine programme *Food And Drink*. He has written for a wide
range of magazines and newspapers and is the author
of *Crafty Cookery* and *Entertaining with Michael Barry*.

CHEESE AND SPINACH PANCAKES

Serves 6

•

10 pancakes, 25 cm (10
inches) or more across
900 g (2 lb) fresh spinach
600 ml (1 pint) milk
50 g (2 oz) cornflour
50 g (2 oz) butter
1 teaspoon Dijon mustard
225 g (8 oz) Gruyère or
Cheddar cheese
salt
freshly ground black
pepper
4 tablespoons Parmesan
cheese

---

*Preparation time: 25 minutes
Cooking time: 25 minutes
Oven: 200°C, 400°F,
Gas Mark 6*

These really are a meal in
their own right, a spectacu-
lar dinner party piece that
will feed six ordinary or
four greedy people. If you
like, cheat a little by buying
some of the excellent ready-
made French crêpe pan-
cakes that are appearing in
the shops. They are sold in
packets of ten and are huge,
38 cm (15 inches) across, so
the dish really looks
astonishing.

1. Wash and cook the fresh
spinach in a very little water
for 5 minutes.
2. Make a cheese sauce by
whisking the cornflour and
butter into the cold milk

and continuing to whisk
regularly as you bring it to
the boil. Add the mustard
and Gruyère, season and
heat for 2 minutes. Mix half
the mixture with the
spinach.
3. On a plate at least
2½ cm (1 inch) larger than
the pancakes, lay a
pancake. Spread it with
three dessertspoonfuls of
the spinach mixture and
put another pancake on
top. Continue doing this,
on and up, finishing with a
pancake. Pour the rest of
the sauce over the top and

104

spread it as if icing a cake.
4. Sprinkle with the Parmesan cheese and bake in a preheated oven for 20 minutes or until heated through and browned on top. To serve, slice the pancakes into wedges like a cake. This needs nothing with it but a fork and a healthy appetite.

From the left: Lamb and fruit kebabs; Cheese and spinach pancakes; Parson

PARSON

Serves 3
●
225 g (8 oz) long-grain rice
1 onion, peeled and chopped
1 level tablespoon mild curry powder
1 tablespoon butter
1 tablespoon flour
300 ml (½ pint) milk
225 g (8 oz) cold cooked turkey, cut into cubes
1 tablespoon olive oil
1 tablespoon chopped fresh parsley

Preparation time: 15 minutes
Cooking time: 25 minutes

This traditional dish was inspired by the spices that were beginning to arrive in Britain from India at the end of the eighteenth century. It has an original spicy flavour.
1. Boil the rice until cooked, drain and keep it hot. Meanwhile, fry the onion with the curry powder in melted butter for 2 minutes.
2. Stir in the flour and add

the milk gradually. Whisk to a smooth sauce. Simmer for 5 minutes, add the turkey, and heat through.
3. Grease a ring mould with olive oil. Sprinkle some chopped parsley on the bottom of the mould and then add the cooked rice. Press it down firmly and cover the mould with a plate. Turn it upside down, give the mould a sharp tap and turn the rice out on to a serving plate.
4. Fill the centre with the Parson and serve immediately.

MICHAEL BARRY AT HOME

SOUR CREAM AND ORANGE RICE

Serves 4-6
•

900 ml (1½ pints) water
dash of lemon juice
1 dash of good quality soy
sauce
450 g (1 lb) long-grain
brown rice
4 tablespoons oil and lemon
dressing
1 medium red pepper,
deseeded and chopped
2 sticks celery, chopped
100 g (4 oz) black raisins
100 g (4 oz) toasted cashew
nuts
100 g (4 oz) lentil sprouts or
any seasonal vegetable
1 bunch spring onions,
chopped
3 medium oranges, peeled
and segmented
300 ml (½ pint) soured
cream
salt
freshly ground black
pepper

Preparation time: 45 minutes,
plus cooling
Cooking time: 30 minutes

---

1. Bring the water to the boil in a saucepan, adding the lemon juice and soy sauce.
2. Meanwhile rinse the rice in cold water to remove any dirt or grains of starch. Add the rice to the saucepan and bring back to the boil. Reduce the heat until the water is simmering and put a tight-fitting lid on the saucepan. Simmer for 25 minutes with the lid on.
3. Turn off the heat and leave the rice in the saucepan for a further 5 minutes

before taking off the lid. Add the oil and lemon dressing while the rice is still hot.
4. Leave the rice to cool and then stir in all the other ingredients, reserving some orange segments for decoration. Season and decorate the salad with the reserved orange pieces and the sour cream.

MARMALADE DUCK

Serves 2
•

1 oven-ready duck
1 orange
100 g (4 oz) marmalade
(dark rather than jelly)
300 ml (½ pint) water
cress (for decoration)

Preparation time: 20 minutes,
plus resting
Cooking time: 1½ hours
Oven: 200°C, 400°F,
Gas Mark 6

I'm obliged to Jane Grigson for this recipe which I've adapted a little from her original. It's the classic combination of duck and orange but not in the classic way! The duck's wonderful mahogany skin and slightly sweet and sour orange flavour will never be connected with the breakfast table.
1. Place the duck in the sink and pour a kettle of boiling water over it. Pat it dry and put half the orange inside. Roast it on a rack over a dripping pan for 40 minutes.
2. Take it out of the oven and pour away the fat. Coat

the duck thoroughly with the marmalade. Pour the water into the dripping pan and put it all back in the oven for 40 minutes.

3. Remove the duck from the oven and leave it to rest in a warm room for 10 minutes before carving. Use the water and marma-

lade dripping to make the sauce, adding the juice of the remaining half an orange. Decorate with cress and serve.

MICHAEL BARRY AT HOME

QUICK PIZZA DOUGH

Makes 3 individual pizzas

•

25 g (1 oz) fresh yeast
1/4 teaspoon ascorbic acid
(vitamin C powder)
450 g (1 lb) flour
1/2 teaspoon salt
300 ml (1/2 pint) hot water
1 tablespoon olive oil

---

*Preparation time: 10 minutes,
plus rising
Cooking time: 15 minutes
Oven: 240°C, 475°F,
Gas Mark 9*

Vitamin C is the crafty quick ingredient here. It's available in powdered form in any chemist. Don't be tempted to use any more than we suggest or to substitute dried yeast. Try spreading the dough with your hands rather than a rolling pin, it's easier and more authentic.

Traditionally, pizza dough takes twelve hours to rise. This version (Neapolitan-approved) takes just fifteen minutes and produces pizzas that are crisp, savoury and subtle. Do heat the oven properly and try preheating the baking sheet or a ceramic tile before putting the pizza on top.

1. Mix the yeast and vitamin C in a little of the water. Add to the flour then mix with all the other ingredients and the rest of the water in a warmed bowl. Knead until smooth.

2. Leave in a warm place to rise for 15 minutes. Knead again, then divide the dough into three balls and spread each ball into a 20 cm (8 inch) pizza base.

3. Spread with Marinara filling (see below) and bake in a preheated oven for 15 minutes, putting the pizzas on a preheated ceramic or metal base in the oven. Eat them hot!

MARINARA

For each pizza

•

2 tablespoons chopped
Italian tomatoes
4 anchovy fillets
6 black olives
1 teaspoon capers
salt
freshly ground black
pepper
1 tablespoon olive oil or
anchovy oil

---

*Preparation time: 4 minutes
Cooking time: see Pizza recipe*

---

1. Spread the tomatoes over the dough, leaving 1 cm (1/2 inch) around the edge. Split the anchovy fillets and arrange them like the spokes of a wheel. Then lay the olives and capers on top. Season lightly. Pour over the oil (using the oil from the anchovy tin is a good idea).

Ragu alla Bolognese

Serves 4

●

225 g (8 oz) lean minced beef
4 tablespoons olive oil
225 g (8 oz) finely chopped onion
1 garlic clove, chopped
50 g (2 oz) chopped chicken livers
50 g (2 oz) grated carrot
425 g (15 oz) tin Italian tomatoes
2 tablespoons tomato purée
salt
freshly ground black pepper
1 teaspoon dried basil
1 teaspoon dried oregano
½ teaspoon thyme

Preparation time: 15 minutes
Cooking time: 1 hour

This is the authentic bolognese sauce. It is very rich and creamy and makes enough to accompany 350 g (12 oz) uncooked pasta.

1. Sauté the beef in the oil until brown. Add the onion, garlic, chicken livers and carrot and sauté for 1 minute more before adding the tomatoes and tomato purée.

2. Then season the mixture and simmer for 45 minutes, adding a little water when necessary to keep the sauce moist. Add the herbs 5 minutes before serving.

From the left: Pizza of Quick pizza dough and Marinara; Ragu alla Bolognese

MICHAEL BARRY At Home

109

APPLE AND SPICE YOGURT

Serves 4

•

4 eating apples
25 g (1 oz) white sugar
1 teaspoon ground
cinnamon
½ teaspoon ground cloves
50 g (2 oz) crystallised
ginger
50 g (2 oz) fine oatmeal
600 ml (1 pint) plain
unsweetened yogurt
4 teaspoons honey
(optional)

*Preparation time: 10 minutes,
plus cooling and chilling
Cooking time: 10 minutes*

This dish is as nice at breakfast as at dinner. For grand occasions, serve it in wine-glasses – it looks very appetising. If you don't make your own yogurt, buy one of the whole milk or goat's milk varieties now available.

1. Peel, core and dice the apples. Simmer them with the sugar, spices and a little (2 tablespoons) of water until they are soft and translucent but not puréed. Leave to cool.

2. Toast the oatmeal under a grill until golden and allow to cool. Mix the apples and yogurt together. Chill for 2 hours.

3. Serve sprinkled with oatmeal and perhaps a teaspoon of runny honey on each portion.

110

BAKED APPLE MERINGUE

Serves 4

●

4 large Cox's apples
2 tablespoons sultanas
2 tablespoons soft brown
sugar
1 teaspoon ground
cinnamon
300 ml (½ pint) apple juice
1 egg white
½ teaspoon cider vinegar
2 tablespoons caster sugar

Preparation time: 15 minutes
Cooking time: 45 minutes
Oven: 180°C, 350°F,
Gas Mark 4

This recipe is served in one of the most highly commended restaurants in Britain where it costs over £7 per portion. It's easy to make, much cheaper and just as good at home.

1. Core the apples without piercing the base. Scoop out the top of each apple and fill with a dessertspoon each of sultanas and soft brown sugar. Sprinkle with cinnamon and place the apples into a baking dish with the apple juice.

2. Whisk the egg white until stiff and add half a teaspoon of cider vinegar. Fold in the caster sugar and beat until smooth.

3. Top each apple with a quarter of the meringue mixture and bake in a preheated oven for 45 minutes.

From the left: Apple and spice yogurt; Baked apple meringue

MICHAEL BARRY AT HOME

111

CHIEN CHIANG

DIM SUM DUMPLINGS

Serves 4-6

•

Dough:
225 g (8 oz) self-raising flour
250 ml (8 fl oz) cold water
1 tablespoon lard
Filling:
450 g (1 lb) minced pork
1 onion, peeled and finely chopped
1 small piece fresh root ginger, peeled and finely chopped
1 tablespoon soy sauce
250 ml (8 fl oz) warm water
pinch of monosodium glutamate (optional)
Sauce:
50 g (2 oz) fresh root ginger, peeled and finely shredded
250 ml (8 fl oz) rice vinegar
120 ml (4 fl oz) dark soy sauce
2 teaspoons sesame oil

Preparation time: 30-40 minutes plus standing
Cooking time: about 15 minutes

---

1. Mix the flour and water together and knead for about 5-7 minutes to make a firm, smooth dough. Allow to stand for 30 minutes.
2. Mix together the ingredients for the filling in a bowl and set aside. Mix the sauce ingredients and put them in a serving dish.
3. Divide the dough into manageable lumps and roll each into a 2.5 cm (1 inch) diameter sausage. Cut into 2.5 cm (1 inch) lengths. Roll each length into a ball, flatten gently, then roll out to 7.5 cm (3 inch) diameter rounds.

has taken the mystery out of Chinese cooking with his popular series on Channel television. He grew up in the Chinese province of Sichuan, famed for its distinctive style of food, and came to Britain at the age of 18 to study at a London printing college. He first visited Jersey on holiday in 1949 and decided to adopt it as his home, establishing a flourishing business, Lu Shan Foods, named after the mountain range of central China, selling a wide range of exotic food and serving delicious lunchtime meals.

---

4. Place a little of the filling in the centre of each dough round. Fold into crescent shapes and pinch the edges firmly together to seal.
5. Heat the lard in a non-stick frying pan. Arrange the dumplings in one layer in the pan and fry for 1 minute or until the bases are golden brown. Add enough water to the pan to come two-thirds of the way up the dumplings. Cover the pan and simmer gently until the water disappears, about 10 minutes.
6. Alternatively, the dumplings may be cooked in a steamer.
7. Serve the dumplings hot, with the sauce.

CRAB AND SWEETCORN SOUP

Serves 4-6

•

600 ml (1 pint) chicken stock
2 × 275 g (10 oz) cans creamed sweetcorn
1 tablespoon sugar
salt
¼ teaspoon monosodium glutamate (optional)
1 × 200 g (7 oz) can crabmeat, drained and flaked
1-2 tablespoons cornflour
3-4 tablespoons cold water

Preparation time: 5 minutes
Cooking time: 10-15 minutes

---

1. Put the stock and sweetcorn in a heavy saucepan and bring to the boil. Add the sugar, salt to taste, monosodium glutamate, if using, and crabmeat. Stir gently to mix, then bring back to the boil.
2. Dissolve the cornflour in the water and stir gradually into the soup to thicken it to taste. Serve hot.

CHICKEN WITH ALMONDS

Serves 4

•

oil for deep frying
75 g (3 oz) blanched almonds
2 tablespoons cornflour
3 tablespoons cold water
175 g (6 oz) boneless chicken breast, skinned and diced
1 tablespoon lard
1 small onion, peeled and diced
1 small carrot, peeled and diced
1 small piece of canned bamboo shoot, diced
5 cm (2 inch) piece of cucumber, diced
50 g (2 oz) canned water chestnuts, diced

1 tablespoon soy sauce
tablespoon rice wine or dry sherry
½ teaspoon salt
pinch of monosodium glutamate (optional)
2 spring onions, cut into 1 cm (½ inch) lengths

CHIEN CHIANG AND ABROAD

Preparation time: 20 minutes
Cooking time: 5 minutes

1. Heat the oil and deep fry the almonds until golden brown. Drain and cool.
2. Dissolve the cornflour in the water. Mix the chicken with a little of the cornflour paste; set the remaining paste aside.
3. Heat the lard in a wok or frying pan and stir-fry the chicken for 1 minute. Add the diced vegetables, soy sauce, rice wine or dry sherry, salt and monosodium glutamate, if using, and cook, stirring, for 2 minutes.
4. Add the spring onions and almonds. Thicken the sauce with the reserved cornflour paste and serve the dish hot.

Clockwise from top right: Dim Sum dumplings; Chicken with almonds; Crab and sweetcorn soup

113

KING PRAWNS, CASHEW NUTS AND YELLOW BEAN SAUCE

Serves 4
•

oil for deep frying
75 g (3 oz) cashew nuts
10 king prawns, shelled and
halved lengthways
1 tablespoon cornflour
2 tablespoons cold water
1 garlic clove, peeled and
crushed
1 tablespoon lard
1 small onion, peeled and
diced
50 g (2 oz) piece of
cucumber, diced
1 tablespoon light soy sauce
1 tablespoon yellow bean
sauce (available in cans)
pinch of monosodium
glutamate (optional)
1 tablespoon rice wine or
dry sherry

Preparation time: 15 minutes
Cooking time: 5 minutes

---

1. Heat the oil and deep fry the cashew nuts until golden. Drain and cool.
2. Remove the black vein from the king prawns. Dissolve the cornflour in the water, add the prawns and garlic and mix together.
3. Heat the lard in a wok or frying pan, add the onion and stir-fry for 1 minute. Add the cucumber and prawn mixture and stir-fry for a further 1 minute.
4. Stir in the soy sauce and yellow bean sauce. Add the monosodium glutamate, if using, and wine or sherry. Cook, stirring, for 30 seconds. Add the nuts, stir to mix and serve hot.

SPECIAL FRIED RICE

Serves 4-6
•

1 tablespoon lard or peanut
oil
1 egg, beaten
1 small onion, finely
chopped
50 g (2 oz) canned water
chestnuts, diced
50 g (2 oz) cooked peeled
prawns
50 g (2 oz) cooked ham,
diced
50 g (2 oz) cooked chicken
meat, diced
350 g (12 oz) cold boiled
rice
100 g (4 oz) frozen mixed
vegetables
1 tablespoon soy sauce
pinch of monosodium
glutamate (optional)
1 spring onion, finely
chopped

Preparation time: 10 minutes
plus cooking rice
Cooking time: about 10 minutes

---

1. Heat a little of the lard or oil in a wok or frying pan, add the egg and cook until lightly scrambled. Remove the egg from the pan and set aside.
2. Heat the remaining lard or oil in the wok and stir-fry the onion and water chestnuts for 30 seconds.
3. Add the prawns, ham and chicken and stir-fry for 2 minutes. Add the rice, vegetables, soy sauce and monosodium glutamate, if using, and stir-fry for 2 minutes longer.
4. Serve the Special fried rice hot, garnished with the scrambled egg and spring onion.

FOUR TREASURES OF THE SEA

Serves 4
•

4 king prawns, shelled and
halved lengthways
100 g (4 oz) rock salmon or
other firm fish fillet
1 small squid, cleaned and
skinned, with tentacles
4 scallops, quartered
3 slices fresh root ginger,
peeled and finely chopped
1 egg white
1½ tablespoons lard
2 garlic cloves, peeled and
crushed
6 dried Chinese
mushrooms, soaked in hot
water for 30 minutes,
drained and quartered
1 very small carrot, peeled
and sliced, or 1 small red
pepper, cored, seeded and
sliced
50 g (2 oz) canned bamboo
shoots, sliced
50 g (2 oz) canned water
chestnuts, sliced
1 tablespoon light soy sauce
½ teaspoon salt
¼ teaspoon monosodium
glutamate (optional)
1 tablespoon rice wine or
dry sherry
2 spring onions, chopped
cornflour and water paste
to thicken

Preparation time: 30 minutes
plus soaking
Cooking time: 5 minutes

---

1. Remove the black vein from the king prawns.
2. Cut the rock salmon into 2.5 cm (1 inch) squares about 5 mm (¼ inch) thick.
3. Make criss-cross cuts on the surface of the squid body without cutting through, then cut into 2.5 cm (1 inch) squares. Cut the tentacles into 2.5 cm (1 inch) lengths.
4. Mix the prawns, rock salmon, squid and scallops with the ginger and egg white.
5. Heat the lard in a wok or frying pan, add the garlic and the fish mixture and cook, stirring gently, for 2 minutes.
6. Add the mushrooms, carrot or red pepper, bamboo shoots and water chestnuts, followed by the soy sauce, salt, mono-sodium glutamate, if using, and wine or sherry. Stir-fry for 1 minute longer.
7. Add the spring onions and a little cornflour paste to thicken. Mix well and serve.

From the top: Special fried rice; King prawns, cashew nuts and yellow bean sauce; Four treasures of the sea

BEEF AND PEPPERS WITH BLACK BEAN SAUCE

Serves 4

•

175 g (6 oz) lean beef
1 garlic clove, crushed
1 tablespoon rice wine or
dry sherry
2 teaspoons light soy sauce
a pinch of M.S.G.
a pinch of black pepper
cornflour and water
50 g (2 oz) lard
1 small onion, diced
1 large green or red pepper,
seeded and thinly sliced
2 teaspoons black bean
sauce (available tinned)

---

*Preparation time: 10 minutes,
plus marinating
Cooking time: 6 minutes*

---

1. Slice the beef across the grain in no thicker than 5 mm (1/8 inch) slices.

2. Mix the garlic, wine, soy sauce, M.S.G., black pepper and a little cornflour paste together; stir in the sliced beef and allow to stand for 15 minutes.

3. Heat 15 g (1/2 oz) of the lard and stir fry the onion for 1 minute; add the sliced pepper and continue stirring for another minute; remove from the pan.

4. Clean the pan and heat the rest of the lard until hot, add the meat mixture and stir quickly, cooking for just one minute or until the colour of the meat changes. Add the onions, pepper and black bean sauce and stir quickly over heat mixing well for approximately 1 minute. Serve immediately.

MIXED VEGETABLES

Serves 4

•

4 Chinese mushrooms
1 tablespoon lard or peanut oil
1 medium sized carrot, thinly sliced
100 g (4 oz) waterchestnuts, sliced
100 g (4 oz) bamboo shoots, sliced
100 g (4 oz) tinned baby corn, quartered
½ teaspoon M.S.G.
salt, to taste
cornflour, mixed with a little water for thickening

Preparation time: 8 minutes, plus soaking
Cooking time: 5 minutes

1. Pour boiling water over the mushrooms and leave to soak for ½ hour; remove the hard stalks and slice the mushrooms.

2. Heat the fat until hot and stir in the carrot for 1 minute then add the remaining ingredients except the cornflour; stir for 1 minute.

3. Add 2 tablespoons of water and simmer for two minutes. Thicken with the cornflour and stir over the heat for one more minute. Serve immediately.

From the left; Beef and peppers with black bean sauce; Mixed vegetables

CHIEN CHIANG AND ABROAD

BAKED WHOLE FISH

Serves 4

•

1 whole fish: bream, bass or
grey mullet, about 1 kg (2 lb)
25 g (1 oz) bamboo shoots,
shredded
2 Chinese mushrooms,
sliced
2 teaspoons soy sauce
2 tablespoons vinegar
2 teaspoons lard
2 teaspoons sugar
2 teaspoons fermented
black beans
$\frac{1}{2}$ teaspoon M.S.G.
1 piece fresh ginger, 2.5 cm
(1 inch) in length, shredded
1 garlic clove, crushed
pinch of pepper

---

*Preparation time: 10 minutes,
plus soaking
Cooking time: 30-45 minutes
Oven: 190°C, 375°F,
Gas Mark 5*

---

1. Soak the Chinese mushrooms in boiling water for
30 minutes before slicing;
discard the hard stalks.
2. Clean the fish inside and
out but leave the head on;
trim off fins. Make cuts on
both sides across the fish to
within 2.5 cm (1 inch) of the
bone, and place in an ovenproof dish. Mix all the ingredients, except for the
lard, and pour this mixture
all over the fish. Top with
the lard cut into small
pieces and bake in a pre-
heated oven for 30-45
minutes. Baste several
times.

Baked whole fish

118

CHIEN CHIANG AND ABROAD

KENNETH LO

PEKING DUCK

Serves 4-6

●

1.5-1.75 kg (3-4 lb) duck
pancakes (see right/left)
5-6 spring onions, cut into
5 cm (2 inch) shreds
1 cucumber, cut into
matchstick shreds
Sauce:
$2\frac{1}{2}$-3 tablespoons
vegetable oil
1×175-225 g (6-8 oz) can
yellow bean sauce
4-5 tablespoons sugar
2 teaspoons sesame oil

---

*Preparation time: 10 minutes
plus drying duck and
making pancakes
Cooking time: $1\frac{1}{4}$ hours
Oven time: 200°C, 400°F,
Gas Mark 6*

---

1. Hang the duck up to dry
in an airy spot for at least
4-5 hours, or if possible
overnight. If in a hurry, use
a hair dryer on it.
2. Place the duck on a rack
in a roasting tin. Roast in a
preheated oven for $1\frac{1}{4}$
hours. Do not open the
oven door during the roasting.
3. Meanwhile, make the
sauce. Heat the oil in a
small saucepan and stir in
the yellow bean sauce. Heat
gently for 2 minutes, then
add the sugar and cook for a
further $2\frac{1}{2}$-3 minutes, stirring. Stir in the sesame oil.
Remove from the heat and
leave to cool.
4. To serve, cut off the
duck's crispy skin and cut
into 5×2.5 cm (2×1 inch)
pieces. Carve off the meat
from the carcase in similar
sized pieces. Arrange the
meat and skin on separate
dishes.

is one of the leading authorities on the possibilities of
Chinese cuisine and has shared his expertise with
Thames television viewers in his *Chinese Cookery
Course*. Born in Foochow, China, he studied physics at
Cambridge and London and pursued varied careers
in diplomacy, fine-art publishing, industrial re-
lations, journalism and lecturing. In 1980 he opened
the Memories of China restaurant in London, which
soon established itself as a favourite with con-
noisseurs. He has written many cookery books.

---

5. To eat, put a spoonful of
sauce on a pancake, top
with meat, skin, spring
onion and cucumber and
roll up, tucking in one end.
Eat with the fingers.

PANCAKES

Makes 24

●

450 g (1 lb) plain flour
$1\frac{1}{2}$ teaspoons caster sugar
250 ml (8 fl oz) warm water
1 teaspoon vegetable oil
a little sesame oil,
for brushing

---

*Preparation time: 20 minutes
Cooking time: about 40 minutes*

---

1. Sift the flour into a mixing bowl and stir in the
sugar, water and oil. Knead
into a firm dough.
2. Divide the dough in half
and shape each portion into
a sausage. Cut each sausage
into 12 equal pieces.
3. Form each piece into a
ball and pat out each ball
into a round. Brush the top
of one round with sesame
oil and place a second
round on top to make a
'sandwich'. Repeat with the
remaining rounds.
4. With a rolling pin, roll
out the 'sandwiches' into
13-15 cm (5-6 inch) dia-
meter pancakes.

5. Heat a dry frying pan
over medium heat and
place one pancake in the
pan. Cook for about $1\frac{1}{2}$
minutes on each side,
shaking the pan so the pancake slides around and does
not stick, or until the pancake begins to puff and
some brown spots begin to
appear here and there.
6. Remove the pancake,
and peel the sandwich apart
very gently. Fold each pancake in half and stack on a
plate. If not for immediate
use, cover with a damp
cloth and reheat in a
steamer.
7. Continue cooking the
sandwiched pancakes as
before.

*Peking duck with pancakes and
accompaniments of sauce,
shredded spring onion and
matchstick cucumber*

KENNETH LO AND ABROAD

121

KENNETH LO AND ABROAD

QUICK-BRAISED GINGER AND ONION CRABS

Serves 4-5
•

3 medium crabs
oil for deep frying
6 slices fresh root ginger,
peeled and shredded
4 spring onions, cut into
5 cm (2 inch) pieces
200 ml ($\frac{1}{3}$ pint) chicken
stock
2 tablespoons soy sauce
$1\frac{1}{2}$ teaspoons salt
3 tablespoons dry sherry
2 tablespoons vinegar
$1\frac{1}{2}$ tablespoons cornflour
4 tablespoons cold water
2 teaspoons sesame oil

Preparation time: 20 minutes
Cooking time: about 10 minutes

1. Remove the main shell from each crab. Chop the body into 4-5 pieces, each with a leg or claw attached. Crack the claws.
2. Heat the oil in a deep fryer or wok. Add the crab, piece by piece, and fry for $2\frac{1}{2}$ minutes. Remove the crab with a slotted spoon, and pour off all but about 1 tablespoon of the oil.
3. Add the ginger and onions to the pan and stir-fry for 30 seconds. Stir in the stock and soy sauce, return the crab to the pan and turn to coat with the boiling sauce. Sprinkle over the salt, sherry and vinegar. Stir-fry for $1\frac{1}{2}$ minutes, cover the pan tightly and cook for 2 minutes.
4. Dissolve the cornflour in the water and add to the pan. Stir until thickened.
5. Sprinkle over the sesame oil and serve hot.

QUICK-FRIED BEAN SPROUTS WITH GARLIC AND SPRING ONION

Serves 4-6
•

4 tablespoons vegetable oil
3 slices fresh root ginger,
peeled and shredded
25 g (1 oz) Szechuan Ja Chai
pickles, shredded
(optional)
3 garlic cloves, peeled and
crushed
2 teaspoons salt
450 g (1 lb) bean sprouts
1 tablespoon lard
2 tablespoons soy sauce
1 tablespoon vinegar
2 tablespoons chicken stock
2 teaspoons sesame oil
3 spring onions, cut into
1 cm ($\frac{1}{2}$ inch) strips

Preparation time: 10 minutes
Cooking time: 5 minutes

1. Heat the oil in a saucepan or large frying pan, add the ginger, pickles, if using, garlic and salt and stir-fry for 1 minute.
2. Add the bean sprouts and stir-fry over high heat for 2 minutes. Add the lard, soy sauce, vinegar and stock and stir-fry for a further 1 minute.
3. Sprinkle over the sesame oil and spring onions and stir-fry for a final 30 seconds. Serve hot.

From the left: Quick-braised ginger and onion crabs; Quick-fried bean sprouts with garlic and spring onion

123

SIMPLE CHOW MEIN OR STIR-FRIED NOODLES

Serves 3-4

•

450 g (1 lb) Chinese noodles
or spaghetti
4 tablespoons vegetable oil
1 onion, peeled and thinly
sliced
2 tablespoons dried
shrimps, soaked for 20-25
minutes and drained
175 g (6 oz) boneless pork
or 4 bacon rashers,
shredded
75 g (3 oz) French beans or
mange-tout
½ chicken stock cube
5 tablespoons hot stock or
water
175 g (6 oz) bean sprouts
2 tablespoons soy sauce
1 tablespoon lard or butter
3 spring onions, cut into
2.5 cm (1 inch) lengths
2 tablespoons dry sherry

*Preparation time: 10 minutes,
plus soaking
Cooking time: about 15 minutes*

1. Cook the noodles in boiling water for 5-6 minutes (or spaghetti for 17-18 minutes) or until tender. Drain and rinse under running water. Set aside.
2. Heat the oil in a large frying pan, add the onion, shrimps, pork or bacon and beans or mange-tout. Stir-fry for 2½ minutes, then add the stock cube dissolved in the stock or water. Stir-fry for 1½ minutes.
3. Remove half the mixture from the pan and reserve. Add the bean sprouts and noodles to the mixture in the pan. Sprinkle over 1 tablespoon of the soy sauce

and stir to mix well. Cook for about 2½ minutes, stirring, until heated through. Turn out onto a warmed serving dish and keep hot.
4. Add the lard or butter to the pan and melt it, then return the reserved mixture to the pan and add the spring onions, sherry and remaining soy sauce. Bring to the boil over high heat and stir a few times, then pour on top of the mixture in the serving dish.

CHAR SIU

Serves 4-5

•

750-800 g (1½-1¾ lb) pork fillet, cut into 5 × 6 cm (2 × 2½ inch) strips
1 cucumber, thinly sliced
3 tablespoons sugar
4 tablespoons vinegar
Marinade:
1½ tablespoons yellow bean sauce (available in cans)
1 tablespoon dark soy sauce
1 tablespoon red beancurd cheese (optional)
2 teaspoons sugar
1 tablespoon dry sherry
1 tablespoon vegetable oil

*Preparation time: 15 minutes
plus marinating
Cooking time: 17-20 minutes
Oven time: 220°C, 425°F,
Gas Mark 7*

1. Place the meat strips in a bowl and add the marinade ingredients. Mix together, then leave to marinate in a cool place for 1-2 hours, turning the strips of meat several times.
2. Meanwhile, toss the

cucumber with the sugar and vinegar and set aside.
3. Drain the meat and place on a rack in a roasting tin. Roast in a preheated oven for 17-20 minutes or until very brown and encrusted with the marinade.
4. Cut the meat across the grain into roughly circular rounds about 5 mm (¼ inch) thick. Lay the slices on a serving dish, slightly overlapping, and surround with the sweet and sour cucumber.

CRISPY SEAWEED

Serves 6-8

•

1 kg (2 lb) spring greens (cabbage)
50 g (2 oz) split blanched almonds
oil for deep frying
1½ teaspoons caster sugar
½ teaspoon salt
¼ teaspoon monosodium glutamate (optional)

*Preparation time: 10 minutes
plus drying
Cooking time: 5 minutes*

1. Separate the cabbage leaves and roll up into a firm roll. Using a very sharp knife, cut the cabbage crossways into the thinnest possible shavings. Wash the cabbage shavings, then leave them to dry in a breezy spot, spread out on kitchen paper towels or in a large colander, for 1 hour.
2. Deep or shallow fry the almonds until crispy. Drain on kitchen paper towels and cool.

3. Heat the oil again until it is about to smoke, then remove it from the heat to cool for 15 seconds. Add the cabbage shavings and stir, then return to the heat and

124

fry for $2\frac{1}{2}$ minutes. Remove from the heat to cool for 1 minute, then return to the heat and fry again for 30 seconds. Quickly drain the fried cabbage shavings on kitchen paper towels.

4. Serve hot, sprinkled with the sugar, salt and monosodium glutamate, if using. Garnish with the fried blanched almonds.

Clockwise, from top left: Simple chow mein or stir-fried noodles; Crispy seaweed; Char siu

MU SHU ROU

•

12 Golden Needles or dried
tiger lily stems
225 g (8 oz) pork, minced
3-4 tablespoons dried
'wood ear' fungi
1 teaspoon salt
5-6 eggs
6 tablespoons vegetable oil
1½ tablespoons soy sauce
1 teaspoon sugar
100 g (4 oz) bamboo shoots,
shredded
1 tablespoon lard
4-5 tablespoons chicken
stock
2 tablespoons dry sherry
3-4 spring onion stalks, cut
into 2.5 cm (2 inch) lengths

---

*Preparation time: 15 minutes,
plus soaking
Cooking time: 12 minutes*

---

1. Clean and soak the tiger
lily stems and wood ears in
water for 10 minutes, and
drain. Add the salt to the
eggs and beat lightly.
2. Heat a wok or frying-pan.
Add 2½ tablespoons oil and
when it is hot add the pork
and stir-fry quickly for 2
minutes. Add the soy sauce,
sugar, tiger lily stems, 'wood
ears' and bamboo.
3. Stir-fry for 3 minutes.
Remove and put aside. Add
the remaining oil and lard
to the pan. Tilt until the oil
and fat covers the whole
surface. Pour the beaten
egg into the middle of the
pan. After 1 minute stir and
scramble the eggs lightly,
then remove the pan from
the heat. When the eggs are
nearly set give them one
more stir and scramble.

*Clockwise from top: Mu shu rou;
Spring rolls; Red-cooked chicken*

4. Now return the pork and
vegetable mixture to the
pan and place it over high
heat. Stir and mix the pork
and vegetables with the
egg, breaking the egg up
into 1 cm (½ inch) pieces.
Add the stock. Stir and turn
for 1 minute and sprinkle
with the sherry and spring
onions. Stir and turn for
another half minute. Serve
hot. (The Mu shu rou is
eaten rolled in pancakes.)

RED-COOKED CHICKEN

Serves 6-8
•

1.5-2 kg (3½-4½ lb)
chicken
6-7 tablespoons soy sauce
5 slices fresh root ginger
1 tablespoon sugar
300 ml (½ pint) water
4-5 tablespoons dry sherry
2-3 spring onions, cut into
2.5 cm (1 inch) pieces

---

*Preparation time: 10 minutes
Cooking time: 2 hours 5 minutes
Oven time: 190°C, 375°F,
Gas Mark 5*

---

1. Parboil the chicken in a
pan of boiling water for 5
minutes. Drain.
2. Place the chicken in a
flameproof casserole and
add the soy sauce, peeled
ginger, sugar and water.
Bring to the boil, turning
the chicken in the sauce,
then cover and transfer to a
preheated oven. Cook for
1¼ hours, turning the
chicken 3 or 4 times.
3. Sprinkle the chicken
with the sherry and spring
onions, then cook for 15
minutes. Serve hot.

SPRING ROLLS

*Serves 5-6
12 pancakes*
•

Stuffing 1:
3½ tablespoons vegetable
oil
3 garlic cloves, peeled and
crushed
2 teaspoons salt
2-3 leaves Chinese cabbage
or lettuce, shredded
4 spring onions, cut into
5 cm (2 inch) lengths
350-450 g (12 oz-1 lb) bean
sprouts
2 teaspoons sugar
1½ tablespoons soy sauce
1 tablespoon lard
Stuffing 2:
3½ tablespoons vegetable
oil
2-3 young leeks, shredded
2-3 young carrots, peeled
and shredded
2 teaspoons salt
3-4 tablespoons stock
4 large mushroom caps,
shredded
3-4 celery stalks, shredded
2 tablespoons soy sauce
2 tablespoons hoisin sauce
1 tablespoon lard
Stuffing 3:
3½ tablespoons vegetable
oil
100 g (4 oz) mange-tout,
shredded
100 g (4 oz) canned bamboo
shoots, shredded
50-75 g (2-3 oz) French
beans, shredded
1 red pepper, cored, seeded
and shredded
1-2 chillies, seeded and
shredded
1 teaspoon salt
3 tablespoons stock
2 tablespoons soy sauce
2 teaspoons chilli sauce
1 tablespoon vinegar
1 tablespoon lard
2 teaspoons sesame oil

*Preparation time: 30 minutes
plus making pancakes
Cooking time: about 15 minutes*

---

1. To make stuffing 1, heat
the oil in a large frying pan
and stir-fry the garlic and
salt over high heat for 30
seconds. Add the Chinese
cabbage or lettuce, spring
onions and bean sprouts.
Stir in the sugar, soy sauce
and lard. Stir-fry for 1½
minutes longer. Turn into a
warmed serving dish and
keep hot.
2. To make stuffing 2, heat
the oil in the pan and add
the leeks and carrots.
Sprinkle with the salt and
stir-fry over high heat for
2½ minutes. Add the stock
and mushrooms and stir-fry
until the liquid has almost
all evaporated. Add the
celery, soy sauce, hoisin
sauce and lard, and stir-fry
for a further 1½ minutes.
Turn into a warmed dish
and keep hot.
3. To make stuffing 3, heat
the oil in the pan and add all
the vegetables and salt.
Stir-fry over high heat for 2
minutes. Add the stock, soy
sauce, chilli sauce and
vinegar and stir-fry for a
further 1½ minutes. Add
the lard and sesame oil and
stir a few more times. Turn
into a warmed dish.
4. Serve the 3 stuffings
with the pancakes. Sauces
can also be served: hoisin
sauce; tomato ketchup
mixed with 2-3 teaspoons
chilli sauce; sesame paste
or peanut butter mixed
with soy sauce and 2 tea-
spoons sesame oil; soy
sauce mixed with 1 table-
spoon English mustard and
½ tablespoon yellow bean
sauce.

127

KEN HOM

RAINBOW BEEF IN LETTUCE LEAVES

Serves 4-6

•

350 g (12 oz) lean beef steak
4 teaspoons rice wine or dry sherry
2 teaspoons light soy sauce
1 teaspoon dark soy sauce
10 g (½ oz) dried Chinese mushrooms, soaked in warm water for 20 minutes and drained (optional)
300 ml (½ pint) vegetable oil, plus 1 tablespoon
25 g (1 oz) bean thread (transparent) noodles
75 g (3 oz) carrots, peeled and cut into 5 cm (2 inch) long fine shreds
50 g (2 oz) canned bamboo shoots, cut into 5 cm (2 inch) long fine shreds
50 g (2 oz) courgettes, cut into 5 cm (2 inch) long fine shreds
½ red or green pepper, cored, seeded and cut into 5 cm (2 inch) long fine shreds
225 g (8 oz) iceberg lettuce, separated into leaves
hoisin sauce, to serve

Preparation time: 20 minutes plus freezing and marinating
Cooking time: 10-15 minutes

---

1. Chill the beef for 20 minutes, then cut it into thin slices about 5 cm (2 inches) long. Put the beef into a bowl and add half the wine or sherry and the light soy sauce. Stir and leave for 20 minutes.
2. If using the dried mushrooms, remove the stalks and cut the caps into 5 cm (2 inch) long fine shreds. Set aside.

and his BBC television series *Chinese Cookery* were 'musts' for lovers of Chinese food who wanted to learn the secrets of successful cooking at home. He was born in the USA to Cantonese parents and food was always very important in his family. From the age of 11 he helped out in his uncle's Chicago restaurant, where he learned the various culinary styles of Chinese cuisine. He now lives in Los Angeles and is well-known throughout the USA and the Far East as a food expert and teacher.

---

3. Heat the 300 ml (½ pint) oil in a deep fryer or large wok until it is almost smoking. Deep fry the noodles until they are crisp and puffed up. Drain on kitchen paper towels and set aside. Allow the oil to cool for future use.
4. Put 1 tablespoon of the oil in a frying pan or wok and heat it, then add the beef and stir-fry for 1 minute. Remove the beef, and wipe the pan or wok clean.
5. Heat 1 tablespoon of fresh oil in the pan or wok and add the carrots. Stir-fry for 1 minute, then add the bamboo shoots, courgettes,

red or green pepper and mushrooms, if using. Stir in the remaining wine or sherry and soy sauce, and stir-fry for 3 minutes.

6. Return the beef to the pan and stir-fry for 1 more minute. Turn the mixture onto a warmed platter.

7. Serve with the noodles, lettuce and hoisin sauce: each guest puts a helping of each ingredient into a lettuce leaf and eats with the fingers.

From the left: Rainbow beef in lettuce leaves; Hot and sour soup; Stir-fried lamb with garlic

HOT AND SOUR SOUP

Serves 4-6
•

75 g (3 oz) boneless lean pork, cut into thin shreds, blanched in boiling water for 2 minutes and drained
25 g (1 oz) dried Chinese mushrooms, soaked in warm water for 20 minutes, squeezed out and drained
25 g (1 oz) bean thread (transparent) noodles, soaked in warm water for 5 minutes and drained
275 g (10 oz) fresh beancurd (tofu), drained and shredded
2 teaspoons sugar
3 tablespoons cider vinegar or Chinese red vinegar
2 tablespoons dark soy sauce
$\frac{1}{2}$ teaspoon white pepper
1 tablespoon cornflour
1 tablespoon cold water
2 small eggs
2 teaspoons sesame oil
2 tablespoons finely chopped spring onions
2 tablespoons finely chopped fresh coriander
1 teaspoon Chinese chilli oil (optional)
Chicken stock:
1 kg (2 lb) uncooked chicken bones (backs, feet, wings, etc.)
350 g (12 oz) chicken pieces
1.75 litres (3 pints) cold water
1 slice fresh root ginger, peeled and shredded
1 spring onion, white part only
1 garlic clove, crushed (unpeeled)
$\frac{1}{4}$ teaspoon salt

Preparation time: 20 minutes plus 2½-4½ hours for making stock
Cooking time: about 3 hours

1. First make the chicken stock. Put the bones and pieces in a large saucepan and pour over the water. Bring to the boil, skimming off the scum. As soon as the stock begins to simmer, reduce the heat: it should never boil. Keep skimming until the stock is clear. This can take 20-40 minutes.

2. Add the ginger, spring onion, garlic and salt and simmer very gently for 2-4 hours, skimming at least twice.

3. Strain the stock through a fine sieve and leave to cool. When cold, remove any fat which has risen to the top. There should be 1.2 litres (2 pints) of stock.

4. Return the stock to a clean pan and bring to a simmer. Add the pork.

5. Discard the mushroom stems and shred the caps finely. Add to the pan.

6. Cut the noodles into 13 cm (5 inch) lengths and add to the pan with the beancurd, sugar, vinegar, soy sauce and pepper. Simmer for 3 minutes.

7. Dissolve the cornflour in the water and add to the soup. Simmer very gently, stirring, until thickened, about 2 minutes.

8. Lightly beat the eggs with half the sesame oil. Pour into the soup in a steady stream, and pull the egg into strands with a fork or chopsticks.

9. Stir in the spring onions, coriander, chilli oil, if using, and remaining sesame oil. Serve immediately.

STIR-FRIED LAMB WITH GARLIC

Serves 3-4
•

350 g (12 oz) lean boneless lamb, such as steaks, fillet or chop meat, cut into thin slices
2 teaspoons rice wine or dry sherry
2 teaspoons dark soy sauce
2 teaspoons light soy sauce
$\frac{1}{2}$ teaspoon sesame oil
2 teaspoons vegetable oil
$1\frac{1}{2}$ teaspoons finely chopped spring onion
3 garlic cloves, peeled and thinly sliced
$\frac{1}{2}$ teaspoon finely chopped fresh root ginger

Preparation time: 10 minutes plus marinating
Cooking time: about 10 minutes

1. Put the lamb in a bowl and add the wine or sherry, soy sauces and sesame oil. Stir and leave to marinate for 20 minutes. Drain, reserving the marinade.

2. Heat a wok or large frying pan. When very hot, add the oil. Add the lamb with a little of the marinade and stir-fry for 2 minutes.

3. Add the spring onion, garlic and ginger and stir-fry for 4 minutes longer. Serve hot.

KEN HOM AND ABROAD

STIR-FRIED MANGE-TOUT WITH WATER CHESTNUTS

Serves 2-4

•

1 tablespoon groundnut oil
3 tablespoons finely chopped spring onions
225 g (8 oz) mange-tout, trimmed
1 tablespoon light soy sauce
2 tablespoons water
½ teaspoon sugar
½ teaspoon salt
1 teaspoon sesame oil
225 g (8 oz) canned water chestnuts, drained, rinsed and thinly sliced

---

Preparation time: 10 minutes
Cooking time: about 10 minutes

---

1. Heat a large frying pan or wok. When quite hot, add the oil and heat this, then add the spring onions and stir-fry briefly. Add the mange-tout and stir-fry for 1 minute.
2. Add the soy sauce, water, sugar, salt and sesame oil and stir-fry for 3 minutes.
3. Add the water chestnuts and stir-fry for a further 2 minutes. Serve immediately.

SICHUAN-STYLE SCALLOPS

Serves 4

•

1 tablespoon groundnut oil
1 teaspoon finely chopped fresh root ginger
2 teaspoons finely chopped spring onion
225 g (8 oz) scallops, including corals
Sauce:
2 teaspoons rice wine or dry sherry
2 teaspoons light soy sauce
1-2 teaspoons chilli bean sauce
2 teaspoons tomato purée
1 teaspoon sugar
1 teaspoon sesame oil

Preparation time: 5 minutes
Cooking time: about 10 minutes

---

1. Heat a wok or large frying pan. When hot, add the oil. Add the ginger and spring onion and stir-fry briefly, then add the scallops and stir-fry for 30 seconds.
2. Add all the sauce ingredients except the sesame oil and stir-fry for 4 minutes or until the scallops are firm and coated with the sauce.
3. Add the sesame oil and stir-fry for 1 minute longer. Serve immediately.

Left: Stir-fried mange-tout with water chestnuts; right, top: Sichuan-style scallops: bottom: Sizzling rice prawns

SIZZLING RICE PRAWNS

Serves 6-8

●

450 g (1 lb) prawns,
preferably raw
1.2 litres (2 pints), plus 2
tablespoons groundnut oil
2 teaspoons finely chopped
fresh root ginger
1 tablespoon finely
chopped garlic
$1\frac{1}{2}$ tablespoons finely
chopped spring onions
Sauce:
1 green or red pepper,
cored, seeded and diced
1 tablespoon cider vinegar
or Chinese black rice
vinegar
1 tablespoon dark soy sauce
1 tablespoon chilli bean
sauce, or 2 dried red chillies
$1\frac{1}{2}$ tablespoons tomato
purée
1 teaspoon light soy sauce
$1\frac{1}{2}$ tablespoons rice wine or
dry sherry
1 teaspoon sugar
300 ml ($\frac{1}{2}$ pint) chicken
stock
1 tablespoon cornflour
1 tablespoon cold water
Rice cake:
225 g (8 oz) long-grain rice
600 ml (1 pint) water
2 teaspoons groundnut oil

Preparation time: 20 minutes
Cooking time: 1$\frac{1}{4}$ hours

---

1. First make the rice cake. Put the rice and water in a 23 cm (9 inch) diameter heavy saucepan. Bring the water to the boil over high heat, then reduce the heat to very low, cover and cook for 45 minutes. The rice should form a heavy crust on the bottom.

2. Remove all the loose surface rice, leaving the crust. Dribble the oil evenly over the crust and cook over a low heat for 5 minutes. The crust should lift out easily at this point, but if it is still sticking, add another teaspoon of oil and continue cooking until the whole thing becomes loose. Put the rice cake on a plate and set aside.

3. Peel the prawns and split them in half, leaving them still attached at the back so that they splay out like butterflies. If using uncooked prawns, remove fine digestive cord.

4. Heat a large frying pan or wok until quite hot. Add the 2 tablespoons of oil and heat until almost smoking. Add the ginger and stir briefly, then add the garlic and spring onions. Stir-fry for a few seconds. Add the prawns and stir-fry for 30 seconds or until firm.

5. Add all the sauce ingredients except the cornflour and water and bring to the boil, stirring. Remove from the heat and add the cornflour dissolved in the water. Bring back to the boil, stirring, then reduce the heat to a very slow simmer.

6. Heat the 1.2 litres (2 pints) of oil in a deep fryer or work until nearly smoking. To test the heat of the oil, drop in a small piece of rice cake: it should bubble all over and immediately rise to the surface. Break the rice cake into pieces and add to the oil. Deep-fry for 1-2 minutes or until puffed and lightly browned. Drain on paper towels.

7. Place the rice cake pieces on a warmed platter and pour over the prawn sauce. It should sizzle dramatically. Serve at once.

FIVE SPICE SPARERIBS

Serves 2-4

•

750 g (1½ lb) pork spareribs
600 ml (1 pint) ground nut oil
Marinade:
1 tablespoon rice wine or dry sherry
1 tablespoon light soy sauce
1 tablespoon cider vinegar or Chinese white rice vinegar
½ teaspoon sesame oil
Sauce:
1 tablespoon finely chopped garlic
1 tablespoon five spice powder
1½ tablespoons finely chopped spring onions
1 tablespoon sugar
1 tablespoon light soy sauce
2 teaspoons finely chopped fresh orange rind
5 tablespoons cider vinegar or Chinese black rice vinegar

Preparation time: 10 minutes plus marinating
Cooking time: 50-60 minutes

---

1. Have your butcher cut the spareribs into individual ribs, and then into chunks about 7.5 cm (3 inches) long.
2. Mix together the marinade ingredients in a bowl, add the sparerib pieces and leave to marinate for about 25 minutes at room temperature.
3. Heat the oil in a deep fryer or large wok. Add the sparerib pieces, in batches, and brown on all sides. Drain on kitchen paper towels.

4. Put all the sauce ingredients in a clean frying pan or wok and bring to the boil. Add the spareribs and simmer gently for about 40 minutes, stirring occasionally. If the sauce is getting too thick, add a little water. Skim off any surface fat and serve hot.

TOFFEE APPLES AND BANANAS

Serves 4

•

25 g (1 oz) plain flour
25 g (1 oz) cornflour
1 large egg
1 tablespoon sesame oil
300 ml (½ pint) groundnut oil
2 large firm apples, peeled, cored and cut into 16 large, thick wedges
2 firm bananas, peeled and cut into 4 cm (1½ inch) chunks
175 g (6 oz) sugar
2 tablespoons white sesame seeds

Preparation time: 15 minutes
Cooking time: about 20 minutes

---

1. Combine the flour, cornflour, egg and 1 teaspoon of the sesame oil in a mixing bowl. Mix to a smooth, very thick batter.
2. Heat the remaining sesame oil with the groundnut oil in a deep fryer or wok. Put the fruit into the batter. Lift out a few pieces at a time with a slotted spoon, draining off excess batter, and add to the oil. Deep fry for about 2 minutes or until golden. Remove with a slotted spoon and drain on kitchen

paper towels. Repeat with remaining fruit pieces.
3. Reheat the oil to moderate and deep fry the fruit a second time for 2 minutes. Drain again.
4. Put the sugar, sesame seeds and 2 tablespoons of the oil in a saucepan. Heat until the sugar dissolves, then cook until the syrup begins to caramelize and turns light brown.
5. Add the fruit pieces to the syrup and stir gently to coat them. Remove them, a few pieces at a time, and drop into a bowl of iced water to harden the caramel coating. Drain and serve immediately.

From the left: Five spice spareribs; Toffee apples and bananas

MADHUR JAFFREY

MASOOR DAL

Serves 4-6

•

200 g (7 oz) split red lentils, rinsed and drained
1 litre (1¾ pints) water
2 thin slices of unpeeled fresh root ginger
½ teaspoon turmeric
1 teaspoon salt
3 tablespoons ghee or vegetable oil
pinch of ground asafetida (optional)
1 teaspoon cumin seeds
1 teaspoon ground coriander
¼ teaspoon cayenne pepper
2 tablespoons finely chopped fresh coriander

Preparation time: 5 minutes
Cooking time: 1 hour 35 minutes

---

1. Put the lentils and water in a heavy pot and bring to a simmer, skimming off any scum that rises to the surface. Add the ginger and turmeric and stir to mix, then partly cover and simmer gently for 1½ hours or until the lentils are tender. Stir every 5 minutes during the last 30 minutes to prevent sticking.
2. Add the salt and stir to mix. Remove the ginger slices.
3. Heat the ghee or oil in a small frying pan and add the asafetida, if using. A second later, add the cumin seeds and let them sizzle for a few seconds. Add the ground coriander and cayenne pepper and stir once, then quickly add this mixture to the lentils. Stir well to mix.
4. Serve hot, sprinkled with chopped fresh coriander.

has made her name as a writer and broadcaster, presenter of the classic BBC series *Indian Cookery*, at the same time as pursuing a successful career as film and stage actress, numbering among her films *Shakespeare Wallah* and *Autobiography Of A Princess*. She grew up in Delhi and first came to London to study at the Royal Academy of Dramatic Art. Since then she has introduced millions to the pleasures of Indian food. She is married with three children and lives in New York.

DO PIAZA

Serves 6

•

4 onions, peeled
7 garlic cloves, peeled
2.5 cm (1 inch) piece of fresh root ginger, peeled and coarsely chopped
450 ml (¾ pint) water
10 tablespoons vegetable oil
2.5 cm (1 inch) cinnamon stick
10 whole cardamom pods
10 whole cloves
1.25 kg (2½ lb) boneless lamb shoulder, cut into 2.5 cm (1 inch) cubes
1 tablespoon ground coriander
2 teaspoons ground cumin
6 tablespoons plain unsweetened yogurt, beaten lightly
¼-½ teaspoon cayenne pepper
about 1¼ teaspoons salt
½ teaspoon garam masala (see page 136)

Preparation time: 15 minutes
Cooking time: about 2 hours

---

1. Halve 3 of the onions lengthways, then cut crossways into very fine slices. Finely chop the fourth onion. Set aside.
2. Blend the garlic and ginger in a blender or food processor with 120 ml (4 fl oz) of the water.
3. Heat the oil in a heavy, wide saucepan and add the sliced onions. Cook until golden brown. Remove and drain on paper towels.
4. Add the cinnamon, cardamom and cloves to the hot oil and cook, stirring, for about 5 seconds. Add the cubes of meat, a few at a time, and brown. Remove each batch as it browns.
5. Add the chopped onion to the pan and cook until just beginning to brown. Add the garlic and ginger paste and cook, stirring, until all the water in it seems to boil away and you see the oil in the pan again.
6. Reduce the heat and add the coriander and cumin. Cook, stirring, for 30 seconds. Stir in 1 tablespoon of the yogurt; when it is incorporated add another tablespoon. Continue, 1 tablespoon at a time.
7. Add the meat with any accumulated juices, the remaining water, the cayenne and salt. Stir to mix and bring to a simmer. Cover and cook gently for 45 minutes or until tender.
8. Stir in the onions and garam masala. Cook, uncovered, for 2-3 minutes longer, stirring gently.
9. Remove from the heat and leave until the fat rises to the surface. Remove with a spoon, then serve hot.

SWEET AND SOUR OKRA

Serves 4-6

•

7 garlic cloves, peeled
1 dried hot red chilli
7 tablespoons water
2 teaspoons ground cumin
1 teaspoon ground coriander
½ teaspoon turmeric
4 tablespoons vegetable oil
1 teaspoon cumin seeds
400 g (14 oz) fresh, tender okra, trimmed and cut into 2 cm (¾ inch) lengths
1 teaspoon salt
1 teaspoon sugar
4 teaspoons lemon juice

Preparation time: 10 minutes
Cooking time: about 15 minutes

---

1. Put the garlic and chilli into a blender with 3 tablespoons of the water and blend to a smooth paste.
2. Empty the paste into a small bowl; stir in the cumin, coriander and turmeric.
3. Heat the oil in a frying pan and add the cumin seeds. As soon as they begin to sizzle, reduce the heat and add the spices. Cook, stirring, for 1 minute.
4. Add the okra, salt, sugar, lemon juice and remaining water. Stir to mix and bring to a gentle simmer. Cover tightly and cook gently for 10 minutes or until tender, adding more water if necessary.

Clockwise from top left: Masoor dal; Sweet and sour okra; Do piaza

TANDOORI-STYLE CHICKEN

Serves 4-6

•

1.25 kg (2½ lb) chicken pieces, skinned
1 teaspoon salt
1 juicy lemon
450 ml (¾ pint) plain unsweetened yogurt
½ onion, peeled and quartered
1 garlic clove, peeled
2 cm (¾ inch) piece of fresh root ginger, peeled and quartered
½ fresh hot green chilli, roughly sliced
3 tablespoons yellow food colouring mixed with ½-1½ tablespoons red food colouring (optional)
lime wedges, to serve
Garam masala:
1 tablespoon cardamom seeds
5 cm (2 inch) cinnamon stick
1 teaspoon black or regular cumin seeds
1 teaspoon whole cloves
1 teaspoon black peppercorns
¼ nutmeg

---

*Preparation time: 30 minutes plus marinating
Cooking time: 20-25 minutes
Oven: 275°C, 500°F, Gas Mark 9*

---

1. Cut each chicken leg into 2 pieces and each breast into 4. Cut 2 long slits on each side of each part of the legs; the slits should never start at an edge and should be deep enough to reach the bone. Cut similar slits on the meaty side of each piece of breast.

2. Sprinkle the salt and lemon juice over both sides of the chicken pieces and lightly rub into the slits. Set aside for 20 minutes.

3. To make the garam masala, put all the ingredients in an electric coffee grinder or spice grinder and grind finely. This will produce 3 tablespoons of garam masala, so store leftover mixture in a small jar with a tight-fitting lid.

4. Blend the yogurt, onion, garlic, ginger, green chilli and 2 teaspoons garam masala in a blender or food processor. Sieve the paste into a large ceramic or stainless steel bowl.

5. If using the food colouring, brush the chicken pieces on both sides with it. Put them into the bowl with the yogurt mixture and add any accumulated juices. Mix well, making sure that the yogurt marinade goes well into the slits in the chicken. Cover and refrigerate for 6-24 hours, the longer the better.

6. Shake off as much of the marinade from the chicken as possible, and put in a large roasting tin in a single layer. Bake in a preheated oven for 20-25 minutes or until just done.

7. Serve hot, with lime wedges.

FRESH CORIANDER CHUTNEY

Serves 4-6

•

½ teaspoon cumin seeds
75 g (3 oz) fresh coriander leaves, coarsely chopped
½-1 fresh hot green chilli, coarsely chopped
1½ tablespoons lemon juice
½ teaspoon salt
freshly ground black pepper

Preparation time: 5 minutes
Cooking time: 3-4 minutes

1. Put the cumin seeds in a small heavy frying pan and roast, stirring, until the seeds turn a few shades darker and give off a roasted aroma. Tip the seeds into a coffee grinder or spice grinder and grind finely. Alternatively, grind in a pestle and mortar.
2. Put the ground roasted cumin seeds in a blender with the remaining ingredients and blend, pushing down with a spatula several times, to a smooth paste.

NAAN

Makes 6 breads

●

150 ml (¼ pint) hand-hot milk
2 teaspoons caster sugar
2 teaspoons dried yeast
450 g (1 lb) plain flour
½ teaspoon salt
1 teaspoon baking powder
2 tablespoons vegetable oil
150 ml (¼ pint) plain unsweetened yogurt, lightly beaten
1 large egg, lightly beaten

Preparation time: about 1 hour plus rising
Cooking time: about 20 minutes
Oven: 275°C, 500°F, Gas Mark 9

1. Put the milk in a bowl and stir in 1 teaspoon of the sugar and the yeast. Leave in a warm place for 15-20 minutes or until frothy.
2. Sift the flour, salt and baking powder into a mixing bowl. Add the remaining sugar, the yeast mixture, oil, yogurt and egg. Mix to a smooth dough.
3. Turn out the dough onto a work surface and knead for about 10 minutes or until satiny. Form into a ball.
4. Pour a very little oil – about ¼ teaspoon – into a bowl, add the ball of dough and roll to coat it on all sides. Cover the bowl and leave to rise in a warm place for 1 hour or until the dough has doubled in bulk.
5. Warm the heaviest baking sheet you have in a preheated oven.
6. Punch down the dough and knead it again. Divide it into 6 equal pieces and keep 5 of them covered while you work with the sixth. Roll this piece into a tearshaped naan, about 25 cm (10 inches) long and 13 cm (5 inches) at its widest point.
7. Slap the naan onto the hot baking sheet, return it to the oven and bake for 3 minutes. It should puff up.
8. Place the baking sheet and naan under a preheated grill, about 7.5-10 cm (3-4 inches) away from the heat, and cook for about 30 seconds or until the top of the naan browns slightly. Wrap the naan in a teatowel to keep warm, and make the remaining naans in the same way.
9. Serve hot.

MADHUR JAFFREY AND ABROAD

From the left: Tandoori-style chicken; Fresh coriander chutney; Naan

LAMB BIRYANI

Serves 6

•

long-grain or basmati rice
measured to the 450 ml ($\frac{3}{4}$
pint) level in a measuring
jug
5.75 litres ($9\frac{3}{4}$ pints) water,
plus 3 tablespoons
about 3 tablespoons salt
1 teaspoon saffron threads
2 tablespoons warm milk
3 medium onions, peeled
4 garlic cloves, peeled
1×2 cm ($\frac{3}{4}$ inch) cube of
fresh ginger, peeled and
coarsely chopped
4 tablespoons blanched,
slivered almonds
200 ml (7 fl oz) vegetable oil
3 tablespoons sultanas
750 g ($1\frac{1}{2}$ lb) boned
shoulder of lamb, cut into
2.5 cm (1 inch) cubes
250 ml (8 fl oz) plain yogurt
5-6 cloves
$\frac{1}{2}$ teaspoon black
peppercorns
$\frac{1}{2}$ teaspoon cardamom
seeds
1 teaspoon cumin seeds
1 teaspoon coriander seeds
2.5 cm (1 inch) piece of
cinnamon stick
about $\frac{1}{6}$ of a nutmeg
$\frac{1}{4}$ teaspoon cayenne
pepper
25 g (1 oz) unsalted butter,
cut into 8 pieces
3 hard boiled eggs, shelled
and at room temperature

---

*Preparation time: 50 minutes,
plus soaking
Cooking time: 2 $\frac{1}{4}$ hours
Oven: 150°C, 300°F,
Gas Mark 2*

Biryanis are grand, festive
casseroles in which partial-
ly cooked rice is layered
over cooked meat. Orange
saffron milk is dribbled
over the top, thereby
colouring some grains
yellow while leaving others
white, and the dish set to
bake in a slow oven.

Soaking the rice in salted
water for long periods, from
3 to 24 hours, gets grains as
white – and as separate
from each other – as
possible. These shining
white grains contrast even
better with those tinted
with saffron.

1. Wash the rice in several
changes of water. Drain it
and put it in a large bowl.
Add 2 litres ($3\frac{1}{2}$ pints)
water and 1 tablespoon salt.
Mix and soak for 3 hours.
2. Put the saffron threads
in a small heavy, preferably
cast-iron, frying pan set
over a medium flame. Toss
the threads about until they
turn a few shades darker.
Put the warm milk into a
small cup. Crumble the
saffron into the warm milk
and let it soak for 3 hours.
3. Cut 2 of the onions in
half lengthwise, and then
cut the halves into fine half-
rings. Set these aside. Chop
the remaining onion very
coarsely. Put this chopped
onion, garlic, ginger, 2
tablespoons of the almonds
and 3 tablespoons water
into an electric blender.
Blend to a paste.
4. Heat 6 tablespoons of
the oil in a 25 cm (10 inch),
preferably non-stick, frying
pan over a medium-high
flame. When it is hot, put in
the onion half-rings. Stir
and fry until brown and
crisp. Remove them with a
slotted spoon and spread
them out on a plate lined
with paper towels.
5. Put the sultanas into the
same oil. Remove them as
soon as they turn plump –
which happens immediate-
ly. Put the sultanas on
another plate lined with
absorbent paper. Put the
remaining almonds into the
oil. Stir and fry them until
they are golden. Remove
them with a slotted spoon
and spread them out beside
the sultanas. Set aside.
6. Now put the meat cubes,
a few at a time, into the hot
oil and brown them on all
sides. As each batch gets
done, put it in a bowl.
7. Add the remaining oil to
the frying pan and turn the
heat to medium. When it is
hot, put in the onion-garlic-
ginger-almond paste from
the blender. Fry, stirring all
the time, until the paste
turns a medium brown
colour. If it sticks slightly to
the bottom of the pan,
sprinkle in a little water and
keep stirring. Return the
meat and any accumulated
juices to the pan. Add the
yogurt, 1 tablespoon at a
time, stirring well between
each addition. Now put in
$1\frac{1}{4}$ teaspoons salt and 150
ml ($\frac{1}{4}$ pint) water. Mix and
bring to a simmer. Cover,
turn the heat to low and
simmer for 30 minutes.
8. While the meat is cooking, finely grind the cloves,
peppercorns, cardamom,
cumin and coriander seeds,
cinnamon and nutmeg in a
spice grinder.
9. When the meat has
cooked for 30 minutes, add
the spice from the grinder
and the cayenne and mix
well. Cover and continue to
cook on a low heat for another 30 minutes. Remove
the lid, raise the heat to
medium, and cook, stirring
all the time, until you have
about 200 ml (7 fl oz) of
thick sauce left in the pan.
Turn off the heat and spoon
off as much grease as possible. The meat should be
cooked by now.
10. Spread out the meat
and the sauce in the bottom
of a heavy casserole. Cover
and keep warm.
11. Bring 3.5 litres (6
pints) of the water to a
rolling boil in a large sauce-

pan. Add 1½ tablespoons salt. Drain the rice and rinse it under running water. Slowly, scatter the rice into the boiling water. Bring to a boil again and boil rapidly for exactly 6 minutes, then drain.

12. Work fast now. Put the rice on top of the meat, piling it up in the shape of a hill. Take a chopstick or the handle of a long spoon and make a hole, 2.5 cm (1 inch) wide, going down like a well from the peak of the rice hill to the bottom. Dribble the saffron milk in streaks along the sides of the hill. Lay the pieces of butter on the sides of the hill, and scatter 2 tablespoons of the browned onions over it. Cover with foil, sealing the edges well, and then with a lid. Bake in a preheated oven for 1 hour.

13. Remove from the oven. If left in a warm place, it will stay hot for 30 minutes.

14. Just before you serve, quarter the eggs, length-wise. Mix the contents of the casserole gently. Serve the rice on a warmed plate, garnished with the eggs, the rest of the onions, the sultanas and almonds.

Lamb biryani

BEEF VINDALOO

Serves 6

●

2 teaspoons cumin seeds
2-3 hot dried red chillies
1 teaspoon black
peppercorns
1 teaspoon cardamom
seeds
7.5 cm (3 inch) cinnamon
stick
$1\frac{1}{2}$ teaspoons black
mustard seeds
1 teaspoon fenugreek seeds
5 tablespoons white wine
vinegar
$1\frac{1}{2}$-2 teaspoons salt
1 teaspoon light brown
sugar
150 ml ($\frac{1}{4}$ pint) vegetable
oil
200 g (7 oz) onions, peeled
and thinly sliced into half
rings
250 ml (8 fl oz) water, plus
4-6 tablespoons
2.5 cm (1 inch) piece of
fresh root ginger, peeled
and coarsely chopped
1 small head of garlic,
separated and peeled
1 kg (2 lb) lean boneless
beef, cut into 2.5 cm (1
inch) cubes
1 tablespoon ground
coriander
$\frac{1}{2}$ teaspoon turmeric

Preparation time: 15 minutes
Cooking time: $1\frac{1}{2}$ hours

1. Put the cumin seeds, red
chillies, peppercorns, cardamom seeds, cinnamon,
mustard seeds and fenu-
greek seeds in a spice
grinder, grind finely and
turn into a bowl. Add the
vinegar, salt and sugar and
stir to mix. Set aside.
2. Heat the oil in a wide,

heavy pot and add the onions. Cook, stirring frequently, until brown and crisp. Remove the onions with a slotted spoon to a blender or food processor. Add 2 tablespoons of the water and purée the onions. Add the onion purée to the spice mixture and mix. (This is the vindaloo paste.)
3. Blend the ginger and garlic in the blender or food professor with 2 tablespoons of water.
4. Heat the oil remaining in the pot and add the beef cubes, a few at a time. Brown on all sides, then remove from the pot.
5. When all the beef has been browned, add the ginger and garlic paste to the pot. Cook, stirring, for a few seconds, then stir in the coriander and turmeric.
6. Return the beef to the pot with any accumulated juices, and stir in the vindaloo paste and remaining water. Bring to the boil, then cover and simmer gently for 1 hour or until the beef is tender. Stir a few times during the cooking.

SPICED BASMATI RICE

Serves 4
●

450 ml ($\frac{3}{4}$ pint) basmati rice
3 tablespoons vegetable oil
50 g (2 oz) onion, peeled and finely chopped
$\frac{1}{2}$ fresh hot green chilli, finely chopped
$\frac{1}{2}$ teaspoon very finely chopped garlic
$\frac{1}{2}$ teaspoon garam masala (see page 136)
1 teaspoon salt
600 ml (1 pint) chicken stock

Preparation time: 10 minutes, plus soaking and draining
Cooking time: 40-45 minutes

1. Wash the rice in several changes of water, then put it in a bowl, cover with 1.2 litres (2 pints) of cold water and leave it to soak for 30 minutes.
2. Leave the rice to drain in a sieve for 20 minutes.
3. Heat the oil in a heavy-bottomed saucepan over a medium flame, add the onion and fry until golden brown. Add the rice, chilli, garlic, garam masala and salt and cook, stirring, for 3-4 minutes to coat all the rice grains with oil.
4. Add the stock and bring to the boil. Cover tightly and cook over a very low heat for 25 minutes or until the rice is tender and has absorbed all the liquid.

KULFI

Serves 6
●

2 litres ($3\frac{1}{2}$ pints) milk
10 cardamom pods
4-5 tablespoons sugar
15 g ($\frac{1}{2}$ oz) blanched almonds, chopped
25 g (1 oz) unsalted pistachio nuts, chopped

Preparation time: 10 minutes plus freezing
Cooking time: about 1 $\frac{1}{4}$ hours

1. Bring the milk to the boil in a heavy pot. As soon as it begins to rise, turn the heat down, adjusting it so the milk will simmer vigorously without boiling over. Add the cardamom pods and simmer until reduced to about one-third of the original quantity. Stir frequently during this process.

2. Remove and discard the cardamom pods. Add the sugar and almonds and stir and simmer gently for 2-3 minutes.
3. Pour the milk into a bowl and leave until completely cooled.
4. Add half the pistachios and stir them into the milk. Cover with foil and freeze.
5. Every 15 minutes, remove the freezing milk and give it a good stir to break up the ice crystals. When the frozen ice milk becomes almost impossible to stir, tip it into a chilled 900 ml ($1\frac{1}{2}$ pint) pudding basin, or into 6 chilled small cups or yogurt cartons. Sprinkle over the remaining pistachios. Cover the basin or cups with foil and freeze until hard.

Opposite from top: Beef vindaloo; Spiced basmati rice; below: Kulfi

141

INDEX

ACKNOWLEDGMENTS

The publishers would like to thank the following who were involved in the preparation of this book:
Photographer Ian O'Leary with stylists Linda Ghiradani, Kate Hardy and Maggie Heinz.
Food prepared for photography by Roz Denny, Kerenza Harries, Anne Hildyard, Jennie Shapter, Michelle Thomson, Rosemary Wadey and Steven Wheeler.
Cover shot: Vernon Morgan

The copyright and original publication details for recipes that appear in this book are as follows:

John Tovey's recipes are reprinted from *Cooking with Tovey*, © John Tovey 1982 and *Entertaining with Tovey*, © John Tovey 1979;
Rev. John Eley's recipes are reprinted from *The Complete Cooking Canon*, © John Eley 1984 and 1985, with the permission of BBC Publications, a division of BBC Enterprises Ltd;
Michael Smith's recipes are reprinted from *Cooking with Michael Smith*, © Michael Smith 1981, published by J. M. Dent and Sons Ltd;
Glynn Christian's recipes are reprinted from *Get Fresh with Glynn Christian*, © Glynn Christian 1982, with the permission of BBC Publications, a division of BBC Enterprises Ltd;
Leslie and Susannah Kenton's recipes are reprinted from *Raw Energy Recipes*, © Fisteba A.G. 1985, with the permission of Century Hutchinson Ltd;
Sarah Brown's recipes are reprinted from *Vegetarian Kitchen*, © Sarah Brown 1984, with the permission of BBC Publications, a division of BBC Enterprises Ltd;
Keith Floyd's recipes are reprinted from *Floyd on Fish*, © Keith Floyd 1985, with the permission of BBC Publications, a division of BBC Enterprises Ltd;
Delia Smith's recipes are reprinted from *Delia Smith's Complete Cookery Course*, © Delia Smith 1978 and 1981, with the permission of BBC Publications, a division of BBC Enterprises Ltd;
Patrick Anthony's recipes are reprinted from *More Recipes to Remember*, © Patrick Anthony, with the permission of Anglia Television;
Mary Berry's recipes are reprinted from *Mary Berry's Complete Television Cookbook*, © Thames MacDonald 1983, with the permission of MacDonald and Co (Publishers) Ltd;
Margaret Lamb's recipes were first shown on Border Television's *Country Kitchen* Series, and are © Margaret Lamb;
Evelyn Rose's recipes are printed from *More Recipes from Look North*, © Evelyn Rose 1977, with the permission of BBC Publications, a division of BBC Enterprises Ltd;
Zena Skinner's recipes are reprinted from *Zena Skinner's Down to Earth Cookbook*, © Zena Skinner 1982, with the permission of Robson Books Ltd;
Grace Mulligan's and Dorothy Sleightholme's recipes are reprinted from *Farmhouse Kitchen I, II, III*, © Yorkshire Television Ltd 1975, 1978, 1982, with the permission of Yorkshire Television Enterprises Ltd;
Shirley Goode's recipes are reprinted from *The Shirley Goode Kitchen*, © Shirley Goode 1986, with the permission of BBC Publications, a division of BBC Enterprises Ltd;
Michael Barry's recipes are reprinted from *The Food and Drink Cookbook*, © Michael Barry, Jill Goolden and Chris Kelly 1985, with the permission of BBC Publications, a division of BBC Enterprises Ltd;
Chien Chiang's recipes are reprinted from *A Taste of China*, © Chien Chiang 1984, with the permission of Channel Television;
Kenneth Lo's recipes are reprinted from *Kenneth Lo's Chinese Cookery Course*, © Kenneth Lo and Thames MacDonald 1982;
Ken Hom's recipes are reprinted from *Ken Hom's Chinese Cookery*, © Ken Hom 1984, with permission of BBC Publications, a division of BBC Enterprises Ltd;
Madhur Jaffrey's recipes are reprinted from *Madhur Jaffrey's Indian Cookery*, © Madhur Jaffrey 1982, with the permission of BBC Publications, a division of BBC Enterprises Ltd.